HEALING FROM EMOTIONAL ABUSE

RECOGNIZE THE HIDDEN NARCISSISTIC RELATIONSHIP. DISCOVER HOW TO RECOVER FROM CHILDHOOD TRAUMA DUE TO EMOTIONAL ABUSE CAUSED BY PERSONALITY DISORDERS AND LIBERATE YOUR SOUL

HOPE UTARAM

Table of Contents

Introduction

⸱⸱⸱⸱⸱⸱

One of the things that you have to realize is that a narcissist does not see the need to seek help from a therapist because after all, they think that there is nothing wrong with them. Recovery is for those who have been through abuse. If you have been or are in a relationship with a narcissist, it is high time that you left and sought help for a professional. It is this kind of support that you need to rebuild your self-confidence and bounce back your self-esteem.

Trust me; you are better than you have ever thought possible. The narcissist might have managed to puncture your self-confidence and even crushed your self-esteem, but most importantly you are just a victim. You are not unworthy like they want you to believe. Finding a health professional that has a specialty in trauma recovery will help you journey through the healing process to recovery. If you are not able to leave the relationship, a therapist can also help you to learn the best ways in which you can communicate effectively with your abuser so that you can set boundaries that they will respect and hence, protect you so that they will no longer take advantage of you.

Here are some of the steps that you will have to go through to help you journey through healing to recovery.

Step 1: Cut contact

Once you have left the relationship, keep at that! Stop maintaining contact with your abuser. The main reason why you went is that the affair was not working for you. Therefore, there is nothing that will happen that makes things feel better. The best way to recover from abuse is for you to block all forms of communications.

If you have joint custody of the children, the truth is, you may not be able to wipe this person entirely from your life. It is therefore advisable to create a strict custom contact. And can only communicate on matters regarding your children using third-party channels only! Otherwise, ensure that you have set up court orders for all forms of agreements.

Think about the extreme trauma bonding, the gross abuse and the addiction that you had to the narcissist. Sometimes the best way is for you to accept that the only way you can recover from such damage is to pull away and cut your losses once and for all. Think of abstaining as a way of protecting yourself from hurt. In other words, each time you initiate contact with your abuser, you are handing them the ammunition to blow you off.

Remember that you lived with them and so they know what your weak points are and how they can wound you even more profound. It is until we heal that you will stop forcing yourself on the narcissist for love or craving them or even justifying to ourselves to give them a second chance when we completely stop contact that we can begin to heal.

Step 2: Release that trauma so that you begin functioning again

If we are going to heal, we have to be willing to reclaim our power. We have to do the exact opposite of what we used to believe; 'I can fix him/her, I will feel better.' Your power belongs inside you. The moment you take your focus away from your abuser that you will be able to channel that power into rebuilding your self-love and paying closer attention to making yourself whole again.

At first, it might seem like understanding who a narcissist is and what they do is essential. But the real truth is that these things cannot heal your internal trauma. What you need to do is to decide to let go of that horrific experience so that you can be. You will begin to rise, get relief and balance again once you have decided to take your power where it belongs-inside you.

Step 3: Forgive yourself for what you have been through

When the insecure and wounded parts of us are still in pain, we often are pushed into behaving like children who are damaged. We are often looking for people's approval and especially from our abuser, we hand our abuser the power to treat us as they see fit. And that's the time you will realize that you have given them all your resources-money, time and health. The most unfortunate thing is that while doing that, you end up hurting the people that matter the most in your life-your children, siblings, parents, and friends.

Yes, it might be hard to forgive yourself from this, but you can do that if you want to rebuild your life and everything that you lost to your abuser. By working through your healing process, you will soon find resolution and acceptance. You can move away from lacking self-love and respect to living a life full of truth and responsibility for our well-being.

You will realize that, when you forgive yourself, you acknowledge that this was all a learning curve and this is the experience you learned, and hence, you are going to use that to reclaim your life. It is when you release your regrets and self-judgments that you can start setting yourself free to realize greatness in your life irrespective of what stage we are. The point when you will begin to feel hope again, hope that will steer you forward into fulfillment and a life full of purpose.

Step 4: Release everything and heal all your fears of the abuser and all they might do next

Do you know what bait to a narcissist is? Anxiety, pain, and distress. One of the thing that can perpetuate another cycle of abuse no matter how we tell ourselves that we have separated from them. It is indeed true that abusers can be relentless. In most cases, they do not like being losers. But one thing that you have to understand is that they are not that powerful and impactful as you may have thought them to be.

They need you to fear and go through pain so that they can function. Once you have healed your emotional trauma, they fall apart. Therefore, it is crucial that you become grounded and stoic by not feeding into their drama; this way they will soon wither away along with their power and credibility with them.

Step 5: Release the connection to your abuser

So many people have likened their freedom from a narcissist to that of exorcism. When we liberate ourselves from the darkness that filled our beings, we are allowing ourselves to detox and let light and life to come in. If that light has to take over the shade, the darkness has to leave so that there is space for something new to come in. In the same manner, it is essential that you release all the parts that were trapped by your abuser so that you can tap into a more supernatural power, the power of pure creativity.

When you disentangle yourself from the narcissist, it is not just about cutting the cord; it is also about releasing all the belief systems that you might have associated yourself with unconsciously. It is only then that you can break free to being a new person and not a target of a narcissist.

Even though it might be tempting to seek revenge on your abuser, this is something that you have to try hard to avoid. Rage has the power of pulling you back into deeper darkness and a game that your abuser is an expert at in the first place. The best form of revenge is one in which you decide to take back your freedom and render your abuser irrelevant.

And is likely going to crush their ego, and they will be powerless that they cannot even affect you. Often are in despair when it hits that you are a constant reminder of their extinction. It is at this point that this ends and your soul contracts to allow love and healing in so that you can be whole again.

Step 6: Realize your liberation, truth, and freedom

Traditionally, we learn that loving ourselves is a very selfish act. However, when it comes to finding liberation and freedom from the hands of our abusers, it is a very critical step that allows us to take in the truth and let it set us free from captivity. Yes, it is something incredibly difficult to do, but it is a necessary step to achieving liberation.

Often, society has taught us that we are treated by others the same way we treat them. However, this is a false premise because we get treatment according to the way we treat ourselves. In other words, the measure of love that we get from others is equivalent to that we feel about ourselves.

Therefore, when we open up to healing and recovery, we are opening the doors for others to love us in reality and more healthy ways than ever before. It is this act that serves as a template by which we teach our children so that they do not carry around unconscious patterns of abuse that were passed to them by our ancestors. Only starts when we decide to take responsibility for our happiness and freedom. We slowly become the change that we would wish to see so that we can let go of being someone's victim and stop handing other people our power.

In other words, we take back our lives by doing everything necessary to aid our inner healing irrespective of what the narcissist does or does not do, something irrelevant either way. It is at this point that we can thrive despite what we have been through and what has happened to us.

Chapter 1

—————— ❧❦❧ ——————

How To Get Comfortable With Yourself

Understanding Your Narcissist

Just like a dark hole, a narcissist is able to get into your life, devour your health emotionally and physically. Most especially, a narcissist is able to take away your sanity and manipulate your sensibilities. The strangest truth about a narcissist is that they are attracted to empaths, yet the two are the extreme opposite of each other. There is this compelling pull that draws these two kinds of people together, which as many believe is the universe's way of maintaining equilibrium. For instance, as a typical empath, you have the intrinsic capability to place yourself in another person's shoes and exert deliberate efforts to help them heal. Whilst doing this for a good cause, you as the empath lack the ability to draw boundaries between helping such people and actually falling into being a victim of their condition through chronic self-sacrifice. On the other hand, the narcissist lives within great traumas and conditions; hence they ideally hide behind an idealized version of themselves. This self-image comes off to you, the empath, as being highly attractive and charming, yet in the real sense, they are highly self-centered and indifferent. When these two extreme characters come together, they form a destructive bond that eventually harms the empath. Both characters collide as they attempt to learn and grow out of their conditions through trial and error. Therefore, it happens that your narcissist is the person who takes advantage of your empathetic nature when your characters collide.

Recognizing the Narcissist

While Narcissistic Personality Disorder is one condition, narcissists come in different forms and kinds. This categorization is based on how the narcissists behave towards others. For one to be known as a narcissist, they have to portray characteristics such as a lack of empathy, a dire need for admiration as well as a magnificent view of themselves.

Also, most of the narcissists display some specific behaviors towards their partners. These include getting rid of people they no longer need or love-bombing their victims. However, narcissists behave differently depending on the severity of the disorder traits within them, and what their external environment has exposed them to. Therapists have for a long time attempted to separate these narcissists into distinct categories and understanding them helps you in owning up to your character traits that attracts narcissists. It would be pointless to be shown how to protect yourself from narcissists without first looking at how different narcissists act within their conscious limits, which will involve hurting you. The more you know them, the more you can consciously act and make decisions concerning your relations with them.

Healthy and Extreme Narcissism

One thing that most people do not know is that there is a continuum from healthy narcissism to extreme narcissism. Whenever we hear of the word narcissism, we associate it with all sorts of negativity. The explanation below changes the narrative and deepens our understanding of the entire phenomenon.

In their assessment of the concept of narcissism, Brummelman et al. (2015) described healthy narcissism (HN) as that which entails the possession of considerable degrees of self-esteem without necessarily being withdrawn from a shared emotional life. Extreme narcissism (EN) was described as that which denies people the ability to have a meaningful relationship because they lack self-esteem. Ideally, healthy narcissism makes one take pride in self-image, beauty and often times the triumph of a tough task. Although this joy in one's beauty and achievement can be momentary, it has a powerful sensation. This narcissism type has been considered helpful in managing one's relationship with others because if you can experience joy in being yourself and the impact you have on the world, then you can easily carry through difficult times. It prevents one from the burnout that most people experience after a series of failures. In the case of a romantic relationship, a healthy narcissist is able to take heartbreaks and disappointments in a reasonable manner. They are able to be reasonable because they feel good about themselves. Usually, healthy narcissism mostly grows as part of child development where children at the young age of 2 begin to feel like the world revolves around them based on the love their parent gives them. As they grow up, such people realize that other people have needs as well, and they continue feeling good about themselves as they accommodate others.

Since extreme narcissism is what this book mostly focuses on, it is important to differentiate between healthy and extreme narcissism. First, as pertains to self-confidence, HN leads to high outward confidence that aligns with reality while EN leads to an unrealistic state of grandiose importance. HN enjoys power and admiration, while EN seeks power at all costs without reasonable reserves. Further, HN has regard for other people's ideas and beliefs and does value them, while EN devalues people without feeling remorseful and has antisocial behaviors. HN has values and workable plans to follow while EN has no particular path and easily changes course due to boredom. HN develops from a considerably stable foundation of love as a child while EN has mostly experienced a traumatizing childhood that conditions them to not be considerate of others.

Extreme narcissists are further put in the following categories based on how they manifest the narcissistic behaviors

Vulnerable Narcissists

Also known as closet, covert, compensatory or fragile, a vulnerable narcissist is one who is shy by nature. Often, they dwell within an inferiority complex that develops from childhood; hence they lack the capacity to trust, love or care for other people. Their emotional state is full of self-unworthiness and hatred. They tend to over-compensate these feelings by looking for other idealized individuals with whom they will feel special about themselves. They use techniques such as guilt-tripping and gas lighting to make their target empath give them sympathy and attention. Their main aim is to reclaim supremacy and command of their lives and to compensate for traumas they have faced before.

Invulnerable Narcissists

Also referred to as the elitist, this is the conventional type of a narcissist, one who is bold and highly un-empathetic. They are the complete opposite to the vulnerable narcissists who suffer from a deep sense of inferiority complex since the invulnerable narcissists tend to believe that they are superior to other people. They seek glorification and pleasure, and they are constantly seeking this kind of attention from people they are in a relationship with. Usually, they can do anything to climb up and dominate another person. They can be described in simple terms as braggers and self-promoters that have a constant dire need to prove they are "superior."

Both extreme types use various narcissistic traits such as manipulating other people to fuel their delusions, unfaithfulness, lack of empathy and criticizing people.

Grandiose

Also referred to as classic or exhibitionist, the grandiose narcissist is a very familiar kind of narcissist, one who considers themselves more influential and important. They capitalize on their achievements and seek admiration from others. They often apply a persona that makes them look appealing and charismatic, and they attract their victims by matching their ambitions and energy with their achievements.

Through their know-it-all attitude, this narcissist is always eager to give their opinions even when it is inappropriate, and the opinions are uninvited. They believe that they are more knowledgeable and skilled than anyone else. They like to be the ones talking as others listen. Also, they are bad listeners because they are always thinking about what they will say next. It is difficult to hold a meaningful conversation with this narcissist.

Also, they have a bullying attitude which makes them want to build up themselves by humiliating other people. Some may appear more brutal in the way they emphasize their superiority.

A bullying grandiose narcissist relies on contempt to prove they are a winner.

Seductive

This is the narcissist who uses the technique of making you feel good about yourself, but with the main goal of making you reciprocate those feelings. They will idealize you to capture your attention and get you having that kind of admiration for them. When you have shown them great admiration, they can manipulate your thinking or give you the cold shoulder.

Vindictive

A vindictive narcissist is one who gets totally irritable once you do not recognize the superiority that they try to assert. They are dangerous to be in a relationship with because they aim at destroying you and blackmailing you using your most precious belongings to prove to you that you are a loser. For instance, one may try to get you fired from work, trash talk you to people who regard you and even turn such people against you.

Malignant (toxic)

The behavior of this narcissist is highly comparable to that of sociopaths. They are never remorseful for their actions and have no regard for moral behavior. They are usually arrogant and have a highly inflated ego. They take pride in outsmarting other people and there is often a lot of chaos around them. If they are not caught by the law, they are a great disturbance to the peace of society. Not only do they seek attention, but they also want all other people to feel mediocre.

Amorous

These are the narcissists who satisfy their worthiness by the number of sexual conquests they have had or how their victims help them elevate their status. Normally, an amorous narcissist puts on a pleasing appearance at first glance and will also use gifts to lure their victim. Once they have met their needs, mostly sexual needs, they quickly dispose of them. These are the ultimate heartbreakers who lack remorse for abandoning people and not putting their needs into consideration.

Subtypes

Besides the above major types of narcissists, there are subsets of narcissists which group them not only by how they manifest their narcissistic behaviors, but which also shows how much they like to draw from a relationship with their victims and how hidden their behaviors are. Learning about them can help you further in identifying them. All the above major types of narcissists can fall in the following categories.

Somatic Versus Cerebral

This describes the feature that the narcissist focuses on gratifying themselves. Both types have to use someone else to make themselves look and feel better. Somatic narcissists focus on their physical appearance and like to feel beautiful above everyone else while cerebral narcissists like to be the informers since they feel like they know it all.

Inverted Narcissists

This refers to the narcissist who is co-dependent and they have to attach themselves to other people for them to feel special. They feel fulfilled especially when they get into a relationship with fellow narcissists and they fear abandonment.

Overt Versus Covert

These subtypes of narcissism differentiate between the nature of the techniques they use to manipulate other people and meet their needs. While both types of narcissists do control others for their advantage, the covert narcissist will mostly use methods that are behind the scenes and they even have a ground for denying their actions. Overt narcissists are more direct, and they pursue their needs without care for being discovered.

Chapter 2

——— ✧✦✧ ———

Knowing The Root Of Your Suffering

Narcissistic abuse can have long-lasting effects on the target of this abuse. These are effects that the narcissist can sometimes be unconscious of or, at the very least, insensitive to. The narcissist does engage in abusive acts because they have a purpose, such as to satisfy their vanity or to manipulate you. But it is also true that the narcissist may not fully understand the effects that their behavior has because they are so self-obsessed and they are not able to connect with people deeply the way that others can.

The idea that the narcissist may not be fully conscious of the effects of their abuse is not mentioned to justify the actions of the narcissist. This aspect of narcissistic abuse is touched on here to emphasize just how out of touch the narcissist is. The narcissist perceives themselves as being set apart from others, so it is almost as if you are a different form of life than they are. Just as the lioness lacks empathy for the wild beast that she slaughters in the savanna, so does the narcissist lacks empathy for the loved one whose emotions they aim to crush because they are unable to escape their inflated self-concept.

The abuse that the narcissist inflicts on others has been touched on in other areas of this book. Narcissistic abuse can include manipulation, blackmail, gaslighting, and belittling. Much of the abuse is emotional in nature, but some forms of abuse can be physical, mental, or designed to isolate. In this chapter, we will explore how narcissistic abuse impacts relationships. We will see that the emotional abuse of the narcissist can leave the individual feeling disconnected, isolated, weakened, and alone.

Emotional Abuse

Emotional abuse is such a powerful tool because it can leave a person weak, vulnerable, and incapable of breaking free without knowing why. Human beings naturally seek emotional connections with other human beings. Although the narcissist is generally unable to form a lasting connection with other people because they do not sincerely value others, they do recognize the value that emotions have in forming a connection, and they are able to use their understanding of emotions and human behavior to their advantage.

For example, in a type of mind control called neuro-linguistic programming or NLP, the practitioner of this art can use cues such as involuntary movements, spoken words, physical proximity, and touch to control the thoughts and perceptions of the person that they are using their tricks on. They can use touching (such as placing a hand on the other person's arm) to induce rapport formation with the other person. They can also use eye contact and subliminal messaging to introduce thoughts in the other person's head.

Although most narcissists have not studied NLP, they also behave in this way. The narcissist knows how to behave to get people to like them and what to say to manipulate them. The emotions of the narcissist may be cut off and inaccessible to their significant other, but they understand emotions well enough to permit them to use the emotions of the other person to their advantage. They know when you are sad; they know when you are happy. They know when you may be feeling confident or when you might be feeling particularly dispirited. The cues that you send the narcissist reveal your emotions to them, and they are tools that permit them to abuse you.

This emotional manipulation can have several impacts on a relationship. It can lead the other person in the relationship to have low self-esteem or experience bouts of emotional whirlwinds, where their emotions are up, down, or uncontrollable. This type of emotional abuse can cause you to feel that your emotional needs are not being met in the relationship, even if the narcissist occasionally says or does things to indicate emotional closeness. This emotional manipulation can also lead you to feel sad, even sadder than you were when you were alone.

Isolation

One of the goals of the words and deeds of the narcissist in a relationship is to isolate the other person. This isolation serves two purposes. One, it places the other person in a situation where they are too weak and emotional to leave the relationship, which gives the narcissist someone to continue to abuse for their vanity. Two, this isolation serves the narcissist's codependency need. They may not value you, but the narcissist still needs you on a certain level. They need the validation that comes from being able to belittle you and abuse you. They need to be in a relationship with someone who agrees to be less than them because it satisfies the inflated self-image that they have created for themselves. Therefore, one of the biggest impacts that narcissistic abuse can have on a relationship is to isolate one of the partners effectively and prevent them from being motivated to leave.

Disconnection

The emotional abuse and isolation of narcissism can leave the target feeling disconnected. Human beings form connections by having meaningful interactions with others. This allows the emotional needs of the individual to be met while the corresponding emotional needs of the other person also are met. This type of emotional bonding lies on a spectrum with empathy. Empathy is a way of being emotionally connected with other people without the need for words.

Because the narcissist is false in their display of emotion, and they use words to deceive and manipulate, the other person in the relationship feels disconnected rather than connected with their partner. They may notice this together with exhaustion or confusion, and this is all related to the inability to form a real connection with a narcissist. Also, the other person in this relationship becomes disconnected from the other important people in their life and society as a whole. This disconnection is perhaps more important because it can discourage the individual from leaving the relationship (and thereby reinforcing the isolation). Working on forming connections with people outside of the relationship with the narcissist is actually an important step in breaking free.

Chapter 3

— ❧❧❧ —

Relaxing With What Is Without Judgement

Although there is no way to be certain why some people are narcissistic (while some are not), Narcissistic Personality Disorder is often associated with traumatic experiences in early childhood. Trauma and abuse seem to cause some children to get stuck psychologically, failing to progress from the early and more self-centered stages of development.

All infants are naturally narcissistic in the sense that they care only about their own needs and are unaware that other people exist separately from themselves. Experts in child psychology believe that newborns initially perceive themselves as omnipotent and unlimited by anything, despite the fact that they are completely dependent on others for all their needs.

Why would a powerless infant think of herself as limitlessly powerful? The newborn can't tell the difference at first between herself and other people. Whenever she needs something, her parents or other caregivers immediately and unfailingly provide what she needs. To a newborn infant, the caregiver seems like an extension of the self, an instrument of her own will. Sigmund

Freud referred to this as "primary narcissism," the natural and healthy narcissism of the newborn baby.

As the infant develops, she slowly discovers that her needs will not always be met instantly. She sometimes has to cry for a while before anyone picks her up or feeds her, but she learns that she can still rely on them to meet her needs consistently. Over time, she comes to realize that her caregivers are separate individuals rather than extensions of herself and that she is not really omnipotent or unlimited. Infantile narcissism develops into an understanding of human relationships based on affection, boundaries, and mutual trust.

Unfortunately, this process doesn't always work out the way it is supposed to. If the infant's needs aren't consistently met, trust, and a sense of healthy boundaries never get the chance to develop. Instead, the powerful self-centeredness of the newborn remains, along with a deep and painful sense of distrust, insecurity, and anxiety.

Healthy Ego

Some psychologists speak in terms of "healthy narcissism" and "destructive narcissism," while others prefer to use the word "narcissism" exclusively for the destructive manifestation of an unhealthy ego. Either way, a healthy sense of self is very different from the toxic and basically false self of the destructive narcissist.

A person with a healthy ego is self-confident, but his self-confidence is consistent with reality and his own place in the world. The narcissist is not just self-confident but grandiose, seeing himself as unique and special compared to other people. He may even believe that normal social rules apply to other people but not to him, or that there should be no reasonable limits on what he can demand from others.

A person with a healthy ego might be comfortable with power and may even enjoy it, but a narcissist sees power as the most important goal in life and will pursue power over others even if it harms them. His ability to empathize with other people is limited or nonexistent, and he relates to other people primarily as objects.

A person with a healthy ego genuinely cares about other people and respects their basic autonomy. A narcissist will express care for others if it seems like the right thing to say at the time but does not respect their autonomy and will take advantage of them without caring how they might be affected.

A person with healthy ego development has a sense of personal values and can follow through with long-term plans. A narcissist has no underlying sense of values and finds it difficult to stay focused on any one thing for long because he gets bored and distracted so easily.

Finally, a person with healthy ego development is usually someone who experienced a balanced combination of support and boundaries in childhood. Most narcissists experienced some combination of childhood damage to their self-esteem along with a lack of appropriate limits or boundaries between self and other.

The narcissist's inner self is basically stunted, trapped in an early stage of development. He wants to hold on to the newborn's illusion of being unlimited and omnipotent but doesn't trust other people to meet his needs unless he can control and manipulate them into doing so. He doesn't really think of other people as separate from himself but sees them as tools for getting his own needs met. Without a healthy sense of self, he can only avoid facing the reality of his situation by controlling others.

The most common cause for this failure to completely develop is neglect and abuse, often at the hands of a narcissistic parent.

Narcissistic Parenting

Narcissistic parents don't treat their children as unique individuals but as extensions of their own self-image. For a narcissist, the child's absolute trust and dependence on the caregiver make them the perfect source of narcissistic supply— that is, until the child begins to develop into an independent person. This is already a difficult task for the child of a narcissistic parent, who may never have experienced the combination of trust and healthy boundaries needed for healthy ego development. Still, most children will begin to develop a sense of self over time despite these barriers.

This is something the narcissist simply cannot allow, so the narcissistic parent interferes with the child's independent development to keep the child dependent on them. Through guilt-tripping, emotional blackmail, undermining, and all the other techniques of control and manipulation, the narcissistic parent prevents the child from ever really growing up.

The narcissistic parent will often pressure the child to get good grades or excel in sports or impress others in some way. Affection and praise depend on high performance and are withheld as a punishment for any mistake. This is because the narcissistic parent sees the child as an expression of his own ideal self, but it can cause the child to see love and affection solely in terms of external validation. Without the experience of being loved for his own sake, the child of narcissistic parents can develop an unhealthy fixation on how other people perceive him.

Narcissistic parents insist on being the center of their children's lives. At the same time, they often belittle and undermine their children, especially for not living up to their own unrealistic expectations. Over time, the child can learn that the only way to get praise and affection from others is to do just what they want at all times without question. They can just as easily learn that the most effective way to deal with others is through guilt-tripping, manipulation, and other head games.

In effect, the narcissistic parent trains the child to perceive the world and human relationships in a dysfunctional way. This doesn't always turn the child into another narcissist, but it is almost always profoundly damaging to the child's self-esteem.

Effects on the Child

Different children react differently to narcissistic parenting, due to differences in individual temperament as well as the presence of other influences in the child's life. For example, the child may be exposed to examples of loving families and healthy relationships outside the home or may have a healthier relationship with one parent than the other. The child may experience emotional support and affection from some other source, leading them to recognize that something is fundamentally wrong with the type of parenting they get from the narcissist.

For whatever reason, many children of narcissistic parents grow up as kind and empathetic people, though they may experience other problems due to their traumatic childhood. However, many children of narcissistic parents do go on to become narcissists as well, creating a cycle that can extend across multiple generations.

In some cases, the child never develops the sense of trust and stable affection most people experience in infancy. Instead, he experiences the world as a place where even the most important caregivers cannot be counted on. The child may grow up to feel empty inside, fearful and insecure in relationships with others, and unable to develop a clear identity of his own.

In an attempt to fill this sense of emptiness and earn love and affection, the child may repress her own feelings and her own needs to concentrate solely on pleasing the narcissistic parent. The child's underlying resentment and anger about the situation are pushed down beneath a pleasing façade, to come out later in other ways.

This façade or mask can become habitual, a "false self" based on what the other person wants to see. The true self underneath is filled with anger and self-hatred, because the child has never been loved for his own sake and believes himself to be unlovable. Over time, he learns to mirror the grandiose and unrealistic self-image of the narcissistic parent, as well as the behaviors of control and manipulation that allow the narcissist to protect and maintain the false self like a suit of armor.

Although narcissistic abuse in childhood is a frequent cause of narcissism, some people may develop into narcissistic adults without necessarily having been abused.

Parenting Styles

According to counselor Diana Baumrind, parenting styles can be divided into three general categories.

Authoritative parents have high expectations for their children, but they also treat them with love and warmth and are generally responsive to their needs. This parenting style is a healthy balance of love and strictness.

Authoritarian parents have high expectations but treat their children without much warmth and are not particularly responsive to their needs. This may seem similar to narcissistic abuse, but Baumrind's parenting typology was intended as a description of normal parenting variations, not abusive extremes. The authoritarian parenting style is demanding and somewhat cold, but not extreme enough to be considered abusive.

Indulgent or permissive parents don't set high expectations for their children. They don't do much to monitor their child's behavior or correct faults instead of giving the child the freedom to develop on his own. Unfortunately, this includes tolerating rude behaviors such as nagging and being selfish, childish traits that can be described as narcissistic. An authoritative or authoritarian parent wouldn't tolerate that kind of behavior, but the permissive parent prefers to ignore it.

Studies have shown the authoritative style to be the most effective style of parenting overall. Children with authoritative parents tend to be more successful and happy in life than children with either authoritarian or permissive parents, who are more likely to suffer from mental health problems and to abuse alcohol and other substances.

Some experts in child psychology have added a fourth parenting style to this list: the "neglectful" style. Neglectful parents are similar to permissive parents in that they fail to set consistent boundaries, but different in that they do not offer the child much warmth or affection. In this version of the list, authoritative and permissive parents are affectionate and warm, but authoritative parents also set standards and boundaries more effectively. Authoritarian and neglectful parents are both relatively cold or distant, but neglectful parents also fail to establish limits or boundaries.

According to a research study by Carrie Henschel in Behavioral Health, the permissive and authoritarian parenting styles were both associated with narcissism in children. Henschel speculated that permissive parents might encourage narcissism by failing to set healthy limits and letting the child get away with demanding and rude behavior. In addition, permissive parents were more likely to praise a child effusively or describe her as "special" regardless of her actual achievements. The combination of being praised as special without really doing anything and not being corrected for mistreating others could be enough to create the grandiose but shallow self-image of the typical narcissist.

Henschel also found that the authoritarian parenting style could produce narcissistic traits in children. Considering the similarity between the high expectations and low warmth of the authoritarian parenting style and the behavior of a narcissistic parent, it makes sense that authoritarian parenting could also tend to encourage narcissism. However, the authoritarian parent's relative coldness is not as extreme and doesn't include the manipulative head games of the narcissistic parent.

Henschel didn't consider the effects of neglectful parenting, but some of the permissive parents in her study might have fallen under that category as well since it was added to the list as a variation on the permissive style. It's easy to see how an emotionally distant parenting style could contribute to narcissism in the child, especially when combined with a lack of boundaries and limits. Children learn how to care for others when their parents care for them, and they learn how to respect boundaries when their parents set limits on acceptable behavior. A child of neglectful parents might not have the opportunity to learn either empathy or respect for boundaries.

Narcissistic Entitlement

Henschel's research into permissive parenting might explain one of the most frustrating aspects of narcissistic behavior—the narcissist's seemingly endless sense of entitlement.

According to narcissistic abuse expert Melanie Tonia Evans, the narcissist feels entitled to get whatever he wants whenever he wants it and perceives any refusal to give him what he wants as a horrible injustice. This can include anything from attention to affection to money to sex—there are no legitimate limits on what he has the right to expect from other people in the eyes of the narcissist. Even though the narcissist treats others as if they have no rights, he expects others to respect his rights at all times.

Evans traces this colossal sense of entitlement to four separate causes, any one of which can produce a narcissist. The first is abuse and neglect, such as the experience of being raised by a narcissistic parent. The second is being raised by overly permissive parents who fail to establish boundaries and never say no. The third is being raised by overly indulgent parents who try too hard to give the child everything he could ever want. The fourth is being raised by parents who put the child on a pedestal, creating an overblown but basically fragile sense of self-worth. The child ends up perceiving herself as being special and better than others, entitled to anything she wants just like Violet Beauregarde in Charlie and the Chocolate Factory.

As Evans pointed out, the act of putting your child on a pedestal like this is also narcissistic, as the child is treated as an extension of the parents' ego. This suggests that parental narcissism may be a factor even when the parent isn't actually abusive. The narcissistic parent uses the child to prop up his own false self and influences the child to see the world in the same way.

Other Factors

Other factors may also contribute to the development of a narcissistic personality. Researchers have found some physical differences between the brains of people diagnosed with narcissistic personality disorder and other people. Narcissistic people seem to have less gray matter in two areas of the brain: the prefrontal cortex and the left anterior insula.

These areas of the brain are associated with the ability to experience empathy for others as well as the ability to regulate emotion. This implies that people with a narcissistic personality disorder may have difficulty keeping their own emotions from spiraling out of control and may also find it hard to empathize with other people's feelings. Quick to feel anger or anxiety and slow to feel empathy, the narcissist may simply be at the mercy of her own emotions.

Of course, it's difficult to say whether these brain differences really cause narcissistic personality disorder or whether they are just one factor among many. For example, having less gray matter in your left anterior insula might not make you narcissistic on its own, but might make you more likely to become narcissistic with the right life experiences. As with many other mental health problems, a narcissistic personality disorder may be caused by a combination of environmental and genetic factors.

Problems Associated with Narcissism

Narcissism tends to go along with other mental health problems and personality disorders. People diagnosed with NPD often suffer from depression. They are also more likely to be diagnosed with Bipolar Disorder, also known as manic depression. The person suffering from Bipolar Disorder will alternate between extremely depressed and manically energetic moods.

People with NPD have high rates of substance abuse issues and are especially likely to abuse cocaine. They have high rates of anorexia and may also have higher rates of other personality disorders, including Borderline, Anti-Social, and Paranoid disorders.

Narcissism is so strongly associated with other mental health issues that counselors usually make a diagnosis of NPD after the patient comes in for some other reason. For example, the narcissist may seek treatment for depression after a breakup caused by his own narcissistic behavior, without any insight into his own role in the breakdown of the relationship. Even though he can tell that something is wrong, he still believes the other person mistreated him rather than the other way around.

Although the narcissist is deeply unhappy and incapable of forming healthy relationships with others, most narcissists are unwilling and unable to see themselves as the problem. Seeking help for narcissism would mean admitting that the narcissist's ideal self is actually fake. Because the narcissist can't bear to do this, he blames everyone else for his problems instead.

The therapist who realizes her patient is narcissistic may make a diagnosis of NPD but will have a hard time making any progress as long as the narcissist continues to cling to the false self. Narcissists in treatment are known for arguing with their therapists, and being stubborn about treatment, impervious to any argument the therapist may present.

Chapter 4

⫷❧⫸

Your Behavior Is A Choice

Just as there are different types of narcissists, there are two distinct types of codependents. These are passive and active codependents, and while both exhibit traits of codependency, they typically present in different manners, typically in regards to their fear of conflict.

Passive Codependent

The passive codependent is quite fearful in general. This is the kind of person who is likely to avoid conflict at all costs and will give in to whatever the enabler requests. These are the ones that are typically found in relationships with narcissists or abusive individuals. Because the passive codependents are so afraid of conflict, they are easy to manipulate into obedience.

Further, passive codependent is far more afraid of being alone. They believe they are capable of manipulating and controlling the narcissists in their life, and they attempt to do so, hoping to manage the situation and retain some semblance of control. These attempts are typically quite covert, and they are quickly found to be unproductive, particularly against the narcissist. After several attempts of trying to control the narcissist and learning that there is no use, the passive codependent typically

36

gives up trying and instead decides to reside passively in the relationship. She still meets the needs of the narcissist on demand, feeling that she is only valuable when she does so, and becoming thoroughly addicted to the relationship, but she never does much to stir up trouble. She is terrified of the consequences of attempting to fight back.

Submissive and stoic, she does not emote much. Her emotional needs are discarded altogether for fear of losing the narcissist if she dares try to care for herself or express displeasure. Instead, she seeks to martyr herself to the narcissist and sits back and allows the relationship to slowly consume her.

Active Codependent

In contrast, the active codependent is a bit more willing to put herself out there. She will attempt more overtly to manipulate her narcissistic partner, and she does not fear conflict in the same way that the passive codependent does. She does not fear the conflict, nor does she fear the pain she will feel in inciting an argument, so she is far more likely to confront the narcissist if she feels she has to.

Active codependents are more manipulative in general. They are willing to do whatever it takes to keep their partners in line, such as appealing to guilt or threatening self-harm if they do not get their way. They will use emotions to get their partners to obey them, or at least try to, and this can sometimes cause issues when partnered with a narcissist, as the narcissist does not care about the emotions of others.

The active codependent, much like the narcissist, is likely to push for instant intimacy and closeness. The active codependent will tell all sorts of intimate details of her life, thinking that it creates further trust and therefore love. Especially if these details pertain to past abuse meant to instill anger toward the abuser, this is an attempt by the active codependent to manipulate. It also creates a victim narrative that can sometimes ensure that the person the codependent is attempting to manipulate decides to act out of pity, which of course, the codependent sees as love.

The active codependent, because she is so likely to use overt manipulation tactics, is likely to be mistaken for a narcissist at first glance. She manipulates others in an attempt to get them to stay close to her, but unlike the narcissist, she is trying to be needed so she can serve the other person, rather than trying to draw in a person to manipulate into doing anything she wants. She, like the narcissist, is attempting to feed her own ego with other people, but she is doing this the opposite way, in which she takes care of the other person to feel better about herself, whereas the narcissist needs to be catered to in order to feel better about himself.

This is how the codependent and narcissist become the perfect enabling pair for each other. They each provide what the other needs in what is almost a symbiotic relationship. The problem is that this relationship involves two people entirely self-serving. The catch is that they are self-serving in ways that happen to balance each other out.

The active codependent believes that she can control the narcissist in some way, and she will attempt to exert that control through the above manipulation tactics. She may even resort to such tactics as withdrawing attention temporarily and other tactics that the narcissist is likely to employ. The problem here is that the narcissist will not respond kindly to such attempts, and the entire situation is likely to escalate into something far more insidious and dysfunctional than the original relationship was in the first place.

Codependency Anorexia

Essentially the last attempt at self-defense, codependency anorexia occurs when the codependent turns off her ability to be harmed emotionally. After a life of living with narcissists, constantly being used to meet narcissists' need for supply, the codependent has a moment of clarity. She realizes that this is her life and that she cannot bear to continue living in that manner.

The codependent realizes, at this moment, that she cannot control that she is attracted to narcissists or other abusers. She sees that every time she has found someone that has seemed perfect, she has been met with abuse not too long after and that she has remained in those abusive relationships for far too long. She realizes that her relationships have involved a revolving door of narcissists and abusers in and out of her life, somehow drawn by her codependency as if it were a beacon advertising her as free to abuse, and she acknowledges that she can no longer put up with the pain any longer.

Rather than continuing to suffer, the codependent decides to instead essentially turn off the emotional side of herself. She shuts off her capacity to feel relationships, withdrawing deeply within herself and essentially swearing off of love and relationships. Rather than risking another abusive or narcissistic relationship, she chooses to instead isolate herself.

Of course, isolating herself comes with its own host of problems. First and foremost is that she never attempts to manage her trauma and baggage she carries with her after what was likely quite a long history of abuse. She does not acknowledge what the problem is and instead dips her head into the sand, refusing to fix the problem. While withdrawing is a sort of coping mechanism, it does nothing to help the codependent with healing.

Further, this only serves to run away from human contact in general. The codependent may be avoiding further narcissistic abuse, but she is also avoiding any sort of meaningful relationships as well. She fails to see that there is real, healthy love out there and instead retreats further away from the romantic world. She removes the option for healthy love entirely. While many people can live without affection or romance in any real form, many people consider doing so something they would never want to do.

The codependent reaches the state of codependency anorexia when she manages to entirely separate her emotional and sexual needs. She decides to withdraw herself from all meaningful human contact. She is intentionally starving herself of love and intimacy in an attempt to protect herself, but along with not healing, she is actually just making her wounds worse. Humans inherently seek out companionship. They crave love and intimacy, and without it, they may begin to suffer very real consequences.

Both mental health and the future ability to create healthy relationships suffer during this state of anorexia, in which the codependent is constantly and consciously avoiding human contact. She sees every point of contact as a possibility for danger, and she frequently does whatever she can to steer clear from even perceived possibilities of danger. For example, if she is out at a holiday party that she was mandated to attend for work, she may attempt to avoid anyone she perceives as someone who may be interested in her. Even the smallest kindnesses would be avoided, as the codependent struggles to identify the difference between love and pity or compassion, and if she feels like she might be at risk of opening herself up to a relationship, she is likely to shrink back behind her barrier she has built up, withdrawing emotionally altogether. She sees being closed off as being safe from harm, and she will retreat to that point at any time she feels vulnerable.

Ultimately, the codependent in the midst of anorexia does not recognize how that deprivation of love and sex can cripple her. She may have avoided hurt, but she has also condemned herself to a lonely life, away from any meaningful connection, and that is not a life that very many people want to pursue. People are hardwired to want to connect with each other, and just because she was hurt before does not mean that she will be hurt again. She can learn to love again if she tries to do so, but she is often too afraid to try.

This can lead to an unhealthy attachment to children or family, as neither of those groups risks relationship harm. Unfortunately, this means that children of codependents who have chosen to starve themselves of love may find themselves enmeshed with their parents, meaning that they are used as support rather than being supported by their parents. This is commonly referred to as emotional incest, in which a parent turns to a child to provide the support that is typically provided by an intimate or romantic partner. The child would be the ear to listen to the parent whenever she was hurting or stressed out, but this only puts the child at risk of becoming codependent as well, as the child learns that his own needs are unimportant when compared to the codependent parent's.

Ultimately, this state of codependent anorexia is harmful to everyone involved. The children of the codependent find their own mental health suffering. The codependent is left behind, lonely, and hurt. There is plenty that the codependent can do in order to ease that pain and begin transitioning back to the world of romance. She can seek therapy. She can be evaluated for mental health issues, such as PTSD after her constant barrage of narcissists and abusers running rampant in her life. She can find support groups meant to show her that she is not alone in her suffering. She can begin opening up to friends and family and slowly expanding her circles. What she should not do, however, is seek out a new relationship before she is ready, which may not be for a very long time. She should, however, remember that love is out there somewhere and that it can be attained without concern for abuse.

Chapter 5

Being An Aware Observer Of Your Life

Narcissistic abuse is insidious, slowly penetrating every part of your life. The longer you feel trapped in the abuse, the more lost you become, until eventually; you are just floating through life, a mere shell of the beautiful, personable individual you were before entangling yourself with a narcissist. Little by little, the narcissist broke you down, until one day, you no longer recognize yourself in the mirror. While narcissistic abuse is incredibly damaging, it does not have to be permanent, and you can recover from its effects, though you may always bear some of the scars left by the wounds. If you feel as though you might be in a narcissistic relationship loaded with abuse, this chapter will provide you with the telltale signs and put names to the various types of abuse you may have faced. Please remember, no abuse is worth tolerating, and no matter what anyone else has said, no one deserves to be abused. You deserve happiness and healthiness, and you can attain it. If you feel as though you are being abused and you need help immediately, do not hesitate to reach out to other people around you, or to call your emergency services or your local domestic abuse hotline. There is help available to you and you do not have to be trapped any longer than you already have been.

Types of Abuse

Narcissistic abuse comes in many different forms, and some of them may surprise you. Many behaviors that you may have seen as controlling or that made you uncomfortable may actually be types of abuse that you have overlooked for too long due to a lack of physical evidence of your abuse. Keep in mind that not every type of abuse has to be physical, and there are many other kinds that can leave far worse scars than a fist can. If you are experiencing any of these, understand that you are well within your rights to leave, and leaving is the healthier option. You are not forced to live in an abusive situation, no matter how afraid of failing to live on your own you may be.

Verbal Abuse

Verbal abuse entails yelling, belittling, or any other type of verbal put-downs. These are said with the intention of tearing you down as opposed to being some sort of negative, but still constructive, criticism, and verbal abuse should not be overlooked just because it does not leave physical marks. This may involve name-calling, insults, telling you how useless you are, criticizing you, attacking you, interrupting you, and any other intentionally harmful use of a voice. Even demands, threats, and sarcasm are forms of verbal abuse. In order to decide if something is a form of verbal abuse, consider the context and whether it was malicious. If contextually, it was said to hurt you, then it is likely verbal abuse. If it was something that put you down but was meant to be of benefit to you, it may not have been.

Manipulation

As discussed in depth, manipulation is one of the narcissist's favorite games. They love to exert control over you, pulling your strings to get their desired results with just the right amount of deniability. Oftentimes, these manipulative tactics are done in a way where it seems harmless to outsiders, but you feel it in your gut that it was hostile or demeaning. Trust your gut reaction.

Emotional Abuse

Emotional abuse involves punishments, threats, intimidation, silent treatment, or other acts that sway your emotions. It is meant to belittle you and keep you in fear. This is intended to trigger the FOG response, keeping you stuck in the loop of fear, obligation, and guilt. It also involves playing with your emotions, such as building you up with love bombing only to suddenly tear that love and affection away in the blink of an eye. Anything that toys with your emotions are a form of emotional abuse.

Physical Abuse

This is perhaps the most obvious of the abuse tactics used by narcissists. Any abuse that physically harms you or keeps you trapped in a form of physical abuse. There may be displays of aggression, such as punching doors or walls, or acts of holding you in place when you want to leave. If the other party's hands are ever on you without your consent, it is physical abuse.

Sexual Abuse

Even in romantic relationships and marriages, sexual abuse is an issue to contend with. Just because you are married or have consented to sexual acts in the past does not mean that your permission is indefinite. Some narcissists will use this in order to keep control over you or to serve their own needs when you are reluctant.

Neglect

Neglect is typically considered in the context of a child with a narcissistic parent, though it could be seen in other contexts too if the narcissist is in a position of providing everything needed to survive but has refused to do so. In the context of children, this can include leaving the child in a dangerous situation or starving.

Financial Abuse

Financial abuse entails withholding all money or the vast majority of the money, and only providing the victim with a small amount, or in some cases, none at all, even if the victim is the one who earned it. This is to keep the victim dependent on the narcissist for everything, enabling easier manipulation in the future. This can be done through threats, theft, or even using your name and private information to take out credit cards in your name and build up debt with them.

Isolation

Isolation involves putting a gap between the victim and anyone that may be a support system for the victim. Your contact with the outside world may be restricted in order to grant the narcissist a more complete control, but also to ensure that the abuse is not discovered.

Signs of Abuse

People who are abused by narcissists often report similar signs and symptoms of the abuse. While not every person will follow this pattern exactly, many people will exhibit some of these symptoms if they have been exposed to systematic and regular narcissistic abuse.

Feeling Detached

Detaching yourself is a form of a defense mechanism called dissociation. In this state, you feel detached from your emotions, and in some cases, your body. It is one of the more defining features of experiencing trauma and is frequently seen in survivors of narcissistic abuse. The mind tries to sequester the traumatic event away in order to try to cope with it, but this can have some serious implications, as you may begin to fragment yourself into multiple pieces just to cope with the abuse you have endured, and you may begin to experience altered levels of consciousness and see effects to your memory.

Walking on Eggshells

Those who have lived through trauma often go out of their ways to avoid anything even remotely associated with the trauma. You may constantly start avoiding people that remind you of your abuser or being careful to avoid saying some of the phrases he used frequently in order to avoid feeling a sense of being triggered. You may begin watching what you do or say around your abuser in hopes of avoiding another bout of abuse, but you likely still are his target. This leaves you feeling anxious most of the time, with that sensation of walking on eggshells as you desperately try to avoid setting your abuser off.

Self-Sacrificing

Through being abused and having none of your needs met for an extended period of time, you have given up on meeting your own wants and needs. Your goals and desires are cast aside in favor of catering to the narcissist, ensuring that you never upset or trigger him in an attempt to avoid further abuse. Ultimately, you are left without ambitions or hobbies, having let your entire self be consumed by the narcissist for his own personal gain.

Health Issues Related to Psychological Distress

Oftentimes, your psychological distress manifests physically. Your weight may have fluctuated drastically, or your body, overwhelmed by stress, has begun to show signs of aging or you find yourself getting sicker than you ever have before. Abuse raises cortisol levels as you stress, which suppresses your immune system. Your sleep is interrupted by trauma, which further raises your stress levels.

Distrustful

After being betrayed so thoroughly by someone you once trusted or loved, you find yourself constantly feeling threatened from all sides. You trust nobody around you and seek to protect yourself by remaining hypervigilant around all others, even when the people around you may have given you no signs that they would harm you.

Self-Harm or Thoughts of Suicide

As depression and anxiety develop in the face of abuse, you may find yourself having thoughts of harming yourself or of committing suicide. You feel as though suicide may be the only real way out of your situation, and find yourself struggling to cope. You get to the point that you feel like death is favorable to living any longer trapped with your abuser. Remember, if you are having these suicidal thoughts, or thoughts of harming yourself, you are having a medical emergency. Please seek help as soon as possible to help yourself stabilize so you can get yourself out of the situation that drove you this far in the first place.

Self-Isolating

While the abuser frequently engages in isolating the victim in order to keep the abuse hidden, the abuse victim also may engage in self-isolation. After feeling shame for suffering through abuse, or feeling as though you have let yourself get into this situation, you may be afraid or embarrassed to let other people know about your situation in fear of having them judge you. Especially in a social climate that seems to favor abusers and blame the victim, you may be afraid of stepping out and asking for help, so you instead turn inward and refuse to see anyone.

Blaming Yourself

It is easy to blame yourself for being stupid enough to get trapped in such a bad relationship in the first place when you find yourself suffering through narcissistic abuse. However, keep in mind that you did not ask to be abused, and you did not deserve it. The narcissist is skilled at manipulating people into seeing what he wants them to see and you fell for it, as did others, and as others will do in the future. This is not a flaw with you; it reflects solely on the narcissist.

Self-Sabotage

Victims of abuse frequently find themselves developing an inner voice that reflects that of their abuser. The victim develops shame related to the situation, and in many cases, self-sabotages due to a perceived sense of worthlessness. Because the abuser has beaten the victim down so much, the victim has come to accept the narcissist's narrative of the world surrounding them.

Living in Fear

Narcissists take offense any time anyone around them is experiencing joy or success, and oftentimes, it is during those periods of success or happiness in which the narcissist escalates, punishing anyone who dares to have something to be happy about. This causes the victim of the narcissistic abuse to develop a fear of success or enjoyment. The fearful disposition also allows for the narcissist to continue to remain the center of attention with less competition.

Protecting the Abuser

Oftentimes, the victim feels some twisted need to protect the abuser from the consequences of such heinous actions. This is a coping mechanism that is meant to help assuage the cognitive dissonance that only someone who has been abused by a person declaring love can understand. The victim may feel as though there is a need to protect the narcissist due to obligation and because the narcissist claims to love the victim. The victim usually takes a share of the blame and says that things are not as bad as they seem due to feeling as though the victim will be unable to survive without the narcissist there to help.

Results of Abuse

Ultimately, even after initially escaping abuse, you may notice the long-lasting effects of living with such a toxic monster. Remember, this is not a reflection of you, but of the abuse, you endured, and it will take time and effort for you to work past these hurdles and become the person you deserve to be. The most frequently noticed behavioral habits after having escaped a narcissist's abuse are echoism and some mental health disorders.

Echoism

In the Greek myth of Narcissus and Echo, Echo was cursed. She was only able to repeat what was said to her last, and as she fell in love with Narcissus, she was only able to repeat what he had said. He did not love her back, and ultimately, cursed to repeat his words; she faded away and died, leaving behind only her voice, which would echo anyone who called out around her.

Like the nymph, Echo, those suffering from echoism fail to develop a sense of self or have that sense of self eroded away. Typically the most empathetic and emotionally sensitive people, those who become echoes feel as though they have left behind their identities. They put their needs last, ultimately developing a fear of having needs in the first place. They feel as though having needs and acting upon them is enough to prove that they are selfish, though that is really just a projection tactic the narcissist has used to convince the victim to forsake her own needs for his sake. Echoism is the ultimate sense of people pleasing, and these people suffer, even after leaving the relationship altogether, as the internalized belief that the victim cannot seek to engage in self-care or have any sort of identity away from the narcissist is ingrained.

Mental Health Issues

Those who have suffered from NPD, especially when it was particularly toxic, may find themselves suffering from other mental health issues. The constant strain of trying to satisfy the insatiable narcissist can develop into anxiety and depression, both of which take their tolls on the individual. Constantly having needs gone unmet and receiving criticism if you dare attempt to voice discontent or that you need something can lead to both anxieties at confrontation or a feeling of depression as you come to believe that the situation is hopeless. Through repeated trauma, you may even develop post-traumatic stress disorder, particularly when the abuse suffered from the narcissist is particularly bad.

Ultimately, leaving a narcissistic abuser is the only true way to avoid harm and protect yourself and your mental health. The longer you are in the relationship, the harder it gets to let go as the trauma-bonding makes leaving seem like an impossibility. Despite the abuse, you feel as though life could not happen any other way, and you find yourself stuck. Remember that you do not have to remain in such a relationship, and leaving is always an option.

Chapter 6

⁕⁕⁕⁕⁕

Mindfulness Meditation Practice
And Its Purpose

When you start to recognize the toxic behaviors that narcissists bring into your life, it's natural to feel turned off and want to get some distance from them. When a victim pulls away from a narcissist, but does not firmly resolve to cut off all connections to them, we call this "Going Low-Contact." For many victims, this is the first small step towards revolutionary changes in their social and professional lives.

Still, for a victim of narcissistic abuse, going Low-Contact is a bit like an alcoholic trying to scale back to two or three drinks per week, rather than embracing full abstinence. In some cases, it is truly the best option for the victim--for example, if you share custody of your child with a narcissist, or if you are financially dependent on their continued positive opinion of you. But even in these cases, it is imperative for the victim to maintain strong boundaries, and be vigilant of all their interactions with the narcissist, so as not to allow any subtle or subtextual abusive behaviors to slip through the cracks.

Remember that for the narcissist, all attention is good attention; they may mislead you to feel, for a time, that you have gained the upper hand in the relationship by listening to your complaints about their behavior, even allowing you to yell to express your frustration, or prompting you to "get even" with them. While you might imagine this to be painful or difficult for them, they may, in fact, enjoy being yelled at, because it proves to them that you are still overwhelmed by the emotions they are inspiring in you. It makes them feel powerful. They might want you to feel that you hold power in the relationship for a short time, but this is usually a tactical trick to reel you back in, and lull you into a false sense of security before they exhibit further abusive behaviors. Their goal is to keep you engaged and enthralled, with more of your energy focused on reacting to the narcissist than on feeding your own well-being.

Is it time for a change?

Victims of narcissistic abuse often feel very uncertain about how to move forward, because they are halfway (or more) convinced that they are the problem, and the narcissist has done nothing wrong. The tactics outlined in chapters five and six work cumulatively to train victims to blame themselves for the abuse they suffer through. They have been told that they are melodramatic; that they are overreacting; that they are imagining things; that they are crazy; and that they, the victims, are in fact the ones who possess an overinflated sense of self-importance.

But if you've found yourself here, reading this book, chances are that you know, somewhere deep in your gut, that this relationship isn't good for you. Maybe you've noticed your personality or physical appearance changing the longer you're exposed to this person; perhaps you're experiencing emotional symptoms that you can't easily explain, like depression, anxiety, social fear, or chronic rage. Maybe you've simply realized that you dread spending time with this person, because the relationship only serves them while draining your energy.

Here is a checklist to review whenever you feel worried that a relationship might have become toxic, but you cannot see a clear solution, or trace the source of the problems within it. If you identify strongly with these feelings, that is a pretty strong indicator that something in the relationship needs to change, or at least be examined with a careful eye. Practice listening to your gut, and honoring your feelings. They are not simply an inconvenience, as the narcissists in your life may have taught you to believe; your emotions are powerful tools that can help you avoid danger, and find true happiness.

You don't know which way is up anymore

This is a common effect of frequent gaslighting. In a relationship with a narcissist, victims are often told that their accurate perceptions of reality are delusional. A narcissist might call their victim an ugly name, and then mere minutes later, deny that this ever happened with enough conviction to actually convince the victim that they imagined the entire incident. If you frequently leave contentious conversations with the potential narcissist in your life feeling like you couldn't summarize the discussion to a therapist or other interested party, this may be part of the reason why. It's highly recommended that you start keeping a journal of these discussions and other incidences of inappropriate or abusive treatment; this will help you to recognize and prevent the narcissist's further attempts to gaslight you and avoid accountability. It will also help you to build more trust in your own judgement, and maintain a stronger resolve when the narcissist attempts to hoover you back into their manipulative grasp.

You find yourself in a defensive position over reasonable requests

Narcissists are experts at blame shifting, which means they are great at making their victims feel self-conscious about the realities of their victimhood. Say, for example, that you are best friends with a narcissist who frequently love-bombs and then discards you, showing up without invitation whenever they need your attention, but then standing you up for agreed upon dinner dates. It is perfectly reasonable for a friend in this situation to express dissatisfaction at being stood up, and ask the narcissistic friend to work on improving in this area of the friendship. But a narcissist could easily react by implying that the victim is somehow emotionally weak for not wanting to eat alone, or for needing their validation. They might even go so far as to blame the aggrieved friend for choosing an inconvenient place or time to meet, or having poor communication skills that prevent them from adequately expressing how important it is to them not to be stood up.

This is an attempt to change the subject, or move the goal post, of the argument. If you find it endlessly frustrating to try and keep these sorts of conversations on topic with a certain person in your life, or find that you're having the same argument over and over again without your needs being addressed or the problematic behaviors changing, take note of this fact and proceed with caution. You should never have to apologize or become defensive when asking for a common courtesy from someone who claims to care about you, so long as the request is made in a respectful manner. When you do, you subordinate yourself and set a precedent for others to treat you as a doormat.

You have to explain the basics to an adult, as though they are a child

Do you remember Bill Clinton's impeachment trial, when the whole nation watched the president of the united states-- presumably a very well-educated and socially savvy individual--

ask to have the word "is" defined and clarified for him? We can't necessarily diagnose the former president as a pathological narcissist, but his behavior in that setting was certainly exemplary of narcissistic argumentation tactics. Narcissists cannot accept blame, express genuine remorse, or handle shame, so they're not above playing dumb or skirting on technicalities in order to avoid facing the consequences of their actions. You may be feeling mentally exhausted if there is a narcissist in your life who routinely puts you in the position to explain the rules of common human decency--for instance, why it's rude to interrupt people, or that it's inappropriate to smile or laugh at someone else's emotional pain--as though the narcissist is a five-year-old who couldn't possibly be expected to know any better. It's important to note that you may also have this experience with people who truly do not know better, such as an individual on the autism spectrum; by contrast, though, a person on the spectrum will likely be able to acknowledge it if these issues have been brought to their attention in the past, even if they have not yet corrected the offensive behaviors, whereas a narcissist will feign complete ignorance.

When you think of them, you feel split in two

Like someone who is head over heels for Dr. Jekyll but terrified of Mr. Hyde, you may feel as though you simultaneously love and hate this person. This is an unfortunate result of the cycle of abuse; for all the negative experiences, there are also extreme highs in the relationship, usually ones that overshadow positive experiences in your healthier, more stable interpersonal connections. You may also feel confused about which side of this person is real: the perfect, blameless, unimpeachable figure that most of the world sees, or the monster who comes out every once in a while to terrorize you and a few other unlucky victims. Finally, you may feel split in two based on your knowledge, from past experience, that dealing with them puts you in a real bind; even when you know you ought to stand up for yourself, or for justice on someone else's behalf, you know you'll be damned if you do and damned if you don't. The narcissist won't listen to reason or tolerate dissent, and even if you are in the right, you're all the more likely to be punished for it.

You feel nervous or anxious about situations that never bothered you before

In a relationship with a narcissist, positive and negative reinforcements are doled out seemingly at random. The only logic that can be applied to the rules in this relationship is that of the narcissist's moment-to-moment desire, so you may be lauded for a certain behavior on one day, and then inexplicably punished for doing the same thing at a later point. This dynamic creates a sense of constant tension in the relationship and anxiety in the victim, who doesn't know what they are doing right or wrong. As such, the victim may develop anxieties around specific triggers--people, places, situations or circumstances--feeling that, although they once were comfortable managing these things, they no longer understand what is expected of them, nor do they know what to expect from the trigger in question. Essentially, the victim learns to associate their negative memories and emotions with the circumstances, rather than with the narcissist who made a normal situation unmanageable for them.

You feel afraid of advocating for yourself

Some people naturally struggle to speak up or be assertive with others, but victims of narcissistic abuse tend to feel a very specific brand of fear in regards to asserting their needs in interpersonal relationships. This is because narcissists treat their lovers, friends, colleagues, and families as inferior beings whose needs are secondary; furthermore, they train these individuals to fear that advocating for themselves is inherently narcissistic and makes them unlovable. Victims don't just feel nervous about speaking up--they are truly frightened that asking for fair and equal treatment will result in a catastrophic loss for them.

Spending too much time with a narcissist can destroy a person's internal barometer for healthy levels of self-esteem, so if you find yourself frequently tolerating intrusions over your personal boundaries and feeling afraid to enforce them, it would be wise to seek out the help of a therapist or counselor. Anyone who is afraid to advocate for themselves might as well have a bullseye painted on their foreheads, as they are extremely likely to fall into imbalanced relationships with even more narcissistic abusers.

You can't remember the last time you said "no"

Narcissists train their victims to be "yes" people. Over time, victims learn that they are only as valuable as their ability to please the narcissist (or their flying monkeys), until they reach a point where they don't just help others because they want to-- the urge to please other people becomes imperative, and failure to please others results in deep, haunting shame. In any relationship, whether it is romantic, platonic, familial or professional, you should feel fully welcome to say "yes" to things you want, and to say "no" to anything that makes you uncomfortable. If this isn't the case, you must recognize that there is no room for coercion or manipulation in healthy relationships, and take whatever steps you must in order to protect your right to give or withhold consent at will.

You feel queasy or uncomfortable when receiving positive attention, or compliments, from others

This attitude can emerge in victims who have existed in a state of endless competition with the narcissists in their lives.

Victims may have been routinely punished by the narcissist for "stealing the spotlight," or grown accustomed to having any praise directed their way negated or invalidated by the narcissist shortly thereafter. This mindset may become so deeply ingrained in a victim's mind that they are still uneasy about receiving positive attention when the narcissist isn't present, and is unlikely to ever hear about the interaction. It can even impact the victim's ability to sustain eye-contact with other people, or to do anything in conversations besides ask questions and listen. This attitude also discourages victims from pursuit of their own goals; they develop a fear of apparent success, because it might make them a target of the narcissist's envy.

You don't know who you can trust

Narcissists like to sow fear and mistrust between their various sources of narcissistic supply, whether they are harem members or flying monkeys. In fact, it may be more important for these people to suspect each other of ill intent than it is for any of them to bear genuine enthusiasm or affection for the reigning narcissist. This prevents their underlings from joining forces to overthrow or expose the narcissist, and creates an atmosphere in which everyone believes the narcissist sees, hears, and knows everything that happens, even when they are absent. Fear and paranoia work to keep victims silent.

You are questioning your values, or regretting morally sound choices you made in the past

It's important for everyone to develop a strong internal moral compass, and to make sure it's defined by personal values rather than based on other people's feelings. Narcissistic abuse can create complex webs of cognitive dissonance within victims, who will be gaslit and told that their well-intentioned behaviors were actually malicious, their emotions are hollow and faked for the sake of manipulation, and their anger or sadness is invalid.

If you are feeling pressure to regret or correct a past behavior that you know in your gut was the right choice, it's important to examine this feeling and question the motive behind the pressure. As an example, if you intervene on behalf of an underdog who is being bullied, and are later made to feel as though this was a self-serving or self-righteous action, you should question these assertions. If you reverse your moral compass and accept these judgements, who does that serve most? Who does it protect? How might things have played out differently without your intervention? The pressure to alter your moral compass may come from a third party, but by asking these questions, you'll usually find that the narcissist in your life benefits most from your abandonment of strong moral values.

Going Low-Contact

When you've determined that a certain narcissist has a negative influence on your behavior and emotional landscape, there is no reason to keep trying to fix what's broken between you. By this point, you have likely tried every trick in the book to encourage them to treat you with compassion and mutual respect. From here on out, make an effort not to waste any more of your breath or time on a lost cause.

You may still need to maintain good standing in the narcissist's book; they may have financial, professional, or spiritual power over you, or they may simply be deeply entangled in your social circle. Even so, reducing the amount of energy and effort that you dedicate to maintaining and improving this relationship can free up an enormous amount of time for you to dedicate to healing and personal growth.

It isn't usually necessary to explicitly state your desire to spend less time with this person. You can simply stop reaching out to them, while still offering polite replies when they get in touch with you. You can also make a slow but deliberate effort to remove yourself from shared institutions or groups, so long as you're not doing yourself a disservice with this action, or engaging in this behavior simply to spite them.

It is generally ill-advised to use excuses, if and when the narcissist takes note of your changing behavior. While it might be tempting to answer their question of "what's wrong?" with a gentle rejection, saying "nothing, I've just been busy lately," or "oh, I'm just having some personal issues with my family," these kinds of excuses will eventually come back to bite you in the rear. The narcissist might feel that they are owed more detailed explanations, and start prying into your business; worse, they will expect your behavior to revert to "normal," meaning you'll resume worshipping them and putting up with abuse, once this excuse has run its course.

A far better alternative is to let the narcissist feel like it was their idea to withdraw energy and attention from the relationship. The best way to inspire them to do that is by becoming a dysfunctional source of narcissistic supply, using the "Grey Rock" technique to deflect the narcissist's attention.

Chapter 7

❧❦❧

Practice Makes Perfect

Lot of times you must have heard that true healing happens only when you forgive and forget truly form the bottom of your heart.

You may also be wondering and thinking about the same because almost all faiths talk about forgiveness as a path to healing, but at the same time, the question arises as to how you can forgive the person who caused you so much harm and whether it is possible to forgive someone who has been responsible for your devastation, especially when they do not acknowledge what they have done.

Another question that can haunt you is whether forgiving is justified given that the narcissist is wrong on so many levels and is a dangerous person to not only you but also society in general.

You are not alone in this battle, and it is completely normal to face these questions. Do not beat yourself up for having these questions, and thinking along these lines does not make you a bad Christian at all. You might have also heard things like not forgiving will make you unspiritual.

The first thing to keep in mind is that this is your journey alone. You have every right to decide what to do, when to do it, and how to do it.

But it is good for you to know that forgiveness is a part of the journey. Once you have forgiven the abuser is when you truly have moved on. I struggled with forgiveness for many years until I met Diane. We connected through a support group and I was immediately drawn to her because she always spoke about her abusive partner who she still was not separated from with kindness. I wondered how someone was able to go through such cruel abuse and not only remain in the marriage but manage to keep such a positive attitude. While I do not advice anyone to remain in an abusive relationship, Diane had made her decision to stick with Tom. I couldn't understand it, but I definitely respected her position. She shared how she applied a principle of forward forgiveness, meaning that she had chosen to forgive him for the past, present and also any hurt he would inflict in the future.

This may sound shocking to you, but the truth is, it helped me to put things that had happened to me in perspective. If I was truly going to put the past behind me, I had to confront my hurt and anger, and be able to say. I forgive him forward.

Forgiveness does not mean that you have to let the abuser know that he is off and welcome him back into your life. I certainly did not do that. But like they say, un-forgiveness is like drinking poison and hoping someone else dies.

Complete forgiveness also means forgiving yourself. A lot of times despite all the healing and the steps people take or even you might have taken, you will realize that in your heart, you are not free yet. This is because while you have been able to implement no contact strictly and have established firm boundaries, you have forgotten one most important thing.

The most important thing in your self-healing journey is forgiving yourself. This is because nothing matters—no therapy sessions, no amount of self-care or pampering can do you any good—if you have truly not forgiven yourself.

Why Must You Forgive Yourself?

You must forgive yourself because of the constant blame you have gone through. A lot of times during the journey, you will be blaming yourself for allowing the narcissist to abuse you, for trusting him even after his true colors were revealed, for becoming addicted to him and seeking him out despite all the harm he has caused you. In a toxic relationship such as the one with a narcissist, the person who suffers the most is you. You were the harshest with yourself, and hence, you need to forgive yourself.

When you forgive truly, you are not releasing the burden of the narcissist, but you are releasing the burden you put on yourself.

By forgiving yourself, you drop the baggage that you have been carrying around, so suddenly you experience freedom. Once this happens, you will realize that you are no longer haunted by the memories, and even if you recollect something from the past, they will not damage you or cause a breakdown.

Self-love and self-forgiveness are the ultimate narcissist's repellents. They work like nothing else.

Forgiveness will also remove the resentment from within that you have been holding for so long. It will cleanse your mind and body and set you free.

Forgiveness also does not mean that you have to forget everything. It is just not possible that you will completely forget everything that has happened to you. There is no way you can completely erase this chapter out of your life. And erasing your memories is not required as well. What is required is that the memories stop having a negative effect on you.

Despite healing from the trauma and even if you have forgiven the abuser, it does not mean that you must forget. Having a memory of the events will help you spot red flags in the future and help you protect yourself. During the healing process, you will eventually move from paranoia that everyone is an abuser to a normal hum being who does not have trust issues, but it always to remember the lessons that you learned, and the most important is the ability to spot red flags from a distance.

Not forgetting will also help you see how far you have come and take note of the stronger person that you are today. It will also make you a wiser person.

Last but not the least if you have survived all the abuse and have managed to heal it means that there is a protective force within you that is guiding you, and you must be proud of that.

Last but not least the entire journey of healing from a narcissist is a spiritual journey more than anything else. This is due to the fact that a spiritual journey is one where you seek reconciliation and education through enlightenment. It is the only journey which allows you to travel within you and discover your soul and mind to attain higher goals.

This journey is unique to each individual, and no journeys are going to be the same.

Healing from a narcissistic abuse forces you to go on a path of self-discovery to answer questions that arise related to anger, why you let the abuse happen, why you still love your abuser etc.

The culmination of this journey is when you have identified the answers to the questions, accepted your internal flaws, and worked on repairing them. This is the reason the healing is more a spiritual process. It is the moment of self-discovery, which will teach you that you are entitled to love and respect.

This spirituality from the narcissistic abuse comes in waves and not at a single point in time. You slowly start realizing that

- you are appreciating all the self-love and care you are giving yourself and also acknowledge that self-care is essential for leading a fulfilled life;

- it is completely fine to be a little "selfish" at times because only when you are happy, it can you lead a happy life, and this happiness comes from within;

- you are extremely comfortable with the boundaries that you have established and no longer feel guilty for enforcing them;

- you no longer have intrusive thoughts about your narcissistic ex, and his presence also does not bother you;

- you are completely in charge of your mental and physical space and will not allow anyone to intrude into them without your permission;

- you start honoring yourself more and stop putting others needs before your needs (you no longer suffer from a savior complex);

- you completely acknowledge that a narcissist cannot be changed and that it is not your job to fix him;

- you do not break down when problems arrive; rather, you start looking for solutions on your own (this is a huge step in the right direction because this indicates that you trust yourself and your judgment something that you would have struggled with in the initial days after the abuse).

In addition to the above, you also understand and accept that whatever happened to you was not a punishment but rather a divine lesson from God. As weird as it may sound, this is the truth. All this was essential for you to discover your true potential and accept yourself. Over time you will realize that these punishments are lessons that will help you overcome all the false beliefs that you have about yourself.

You will change from being a codependent person who also needed approval and feared rejection of a confident individual who is not dependent on anyone's approval. The narcissist will cease to have any control or power over, and no reaction will become a routine for you, not something that you need to practice carefully.

You will also realize that transformation is the only way to living your best life, and this is the key to leading your life in an emotionally fulfilling manner. This does not mean that you will never face any problems in life again or that life will be a bed of roses. This means that with the transformation that has taken place, you will be able to tackle the problems in a calm and matured manner with all the new strength that you have acquired.

Spiritual healing is the healing of your "inner spirit." It is the process of working on the life force energy within you and getting back this energy that belongs to you.

Another important learning is that from a spiritual perspective there are no victims. During the initial phase of recovery, everything seems so difficult because you consider yourself as a victim.

Considering yourself a victim will not help you grow stronger; it will rather make you weaker. This is because for centuries, society has considered victims to be weak, and victims have always been associated with weakness. You also must have grown up thinking the same. As long as you feel weak, you can never heal and move forward.

But in spirituality, there are no victims. You will come to understand this as your healing journey progresses. You will understand that each of the events that happened to you was just experiences. The abuse was also an experience that you allowed to happen at some level. You start considering the abused person as a teacher and your experience as a learning experience that taught you a lot about yourself.

You learn intuition from this experience and trust early warning signs. It is not that you would not have experienced early warning signs during the initial stages of the relationship, but you consciously decide to ignore them—you push them away and stop giving your intuition the attention that it deserves. Through the healing process, you start learning to trust your intuition again. Once you start trusting your intuition, you are no longer in a dangerous position where you will fall for a predator such as a narcissist.

You were in a dangerous situation when you were a victim. Because when you are a victim, you lack self-worth and hence attract the wrong kind of people into your life. This danger will continue forever, and there may be chances where you will move from an abusive relationship to another, and the cycle will continue.

The secret for this cycle of abuse to stop is healing from inside. The truth is though abuse happens from the outside, your inner soul gets damaged, and hence, the healing must happen inside. When you are fully empowered, you stop acting like a victim because you no longer feel like one. This automatically will prevent you from falling for abusers such as a narcissist in future because you will walk away as soon as you spot the first sign of a narcissist or any other abuser.

Spiritual healing will also help you understand that your past served a purpose in life and taught you whatever you needed to survive the future. Now that the purpose is over, the past left you, and you must be grateful for the lessons that past taught and also grateful to God that you do not have to live that fearful and traumatic life anymore. So how does one attain spiritual healing? I would say it is simply by drawing closer to God and engaging in spiritual activities like prayer, fasting, studying the bible and meditating on God's promises. You might not feel strong enough to pray for long hours and that is not the point. What is most important is that you spend time talking to him, just like he was seating in the room with you and pouring out your heart to him.

Listening to spiritual songs also have a way of calming me personally, so on the days where I felt too overwhelmed to pray, I just played some music on my phone, over and over. The peace that comes from God is like no other, there is no way I would have made it out with my sanity intact without the help of God.

Chapter 8

⋘⋙

Children In The Narcissistic Relationship

Knowing what you have learned about narcissism, you might wonder why a narcissist would have a child in the first place, considering their desire to be taken care of and adored, rather than care for someone and tend to their every need, especially that of a child who needs a great deal of praise and attention.

People have children, whether they are narcissists or not. It doesn't depend on something like that when you and your partner decide to start a family. A narcissist might enjoy having a child or more than one because it creates an immediate relationship with someone in which they will always have power and authority. In the parent-child relationship, in the opinion of the narcissist, the child will always be beneath them because of the nature of their relationship and their difference in age and life experience.

Sadly, and unfortunately, for the child of the narcissist, they will quickly learn that they exist to please and serve the parent, rather than the parent meeting all of the needs of the child first. The child of the narcissist is there to serve as a healthy reflection of their accomplishments, achievements, and overall perfection.

Just as narcissistic abuse can occur in a romantic partnership, it can also occur in the parent-child dynamics. A young child with a narcissistic parent will learn that they must act and behave as the reflection of their parent, including fitting into behavior and/or mold of personality that is dictated by the parent. It can cause a great deal of anxiety in the child starting at a very early age because they are being persuaded to deny their unique personality to be the mirror reflection that the narcissistic parent desperately needs them to be.

Failure to comply with the wishes of the narcissistic parent, for example, if the child wants to create and set their life goals, the parent will display actions of covert and overt punishment, including avoiding, ignoring, denying, and rejecting the child for a while. The parent will see their child's autonomy as a slight against them as if the child was intentionally betraying them.

A narcissistic parent is hard for a child to understand or trust. They are unpredictable and often confusing, rarely consistent in any direction with their attitudes toward their child or partner. The narcissist is impulsive, unpredictable, and capricious. A child wants stability, trust, and an ability to feel safe as they learn to explore the world.

An inability to understand or make sense of the interpersonal "stunts" of the narcissistic parent can lead to the child internalizing feelings of shame, blame, or guilt when they don't live up to the parent's expectations. This can look a lot like what you read in the last section about the symptoms of narcissistic abuse, in which the child will assume that it is their fault that their parent is unhappy and that they should feel bad as a result of it. A narcissistic parent is completely oblivious to the harm and damage they are causing their child. The message the child receives is basically, "you are only worthy of love if you comply with my expectations and wishes of you."

Commonly, all of these issues are reflected as the child of the narcissist grows up and starts attempting to have relationships of their own. It is in adulthood that they begin to process the trauma of what their narcissistic parent caused them as a developing person.

Children of Narcissists as Adults

A distorted child-parent relationship can create a lot of serious emotional and mental issues as you get older and work on having your relationship experiences. Children of narcissists will tend to seek out or gravitate toward challenging or dramatic relationships because it was what was modeled for them as a child. It is what they know love to "look like." Growing up with the belief that you are not essentially good or lovable, causes the issue of only seeking out partnerships that will perpetuate that belief with another partner.

It is rather common for any child, whether they are in a narcissistic child-parent relationship or not, to seek out relationships in their adult life that replay what they learned in childhood. Asking for something else feels foreign and strange. Imagine a fish out of the water like the child of a narcissist receiving unconditional love from a partner, without expecting anything in return.

Children of narcissists will seek out romantic partners who are critical or judgmental, emotionally distant or unavailable, or who will withhold or deny affection and intimacy. Essentially, they will be looking for a partner who feels comfortable and what they know and understand, replaying the dynamics they shared with their narcissistic/codependent parents.

Of course, anyone can heal from such an experience, and sometimes, a child of a narcissist will find that through some therapy and a few healthy partnerships, they can realize, identify, and defy the issues of their childhood experience with their narcissistic parent. Being able to identify the causes of why you may have issues in your adult relationships often stems from identifying what kind of relationship you had with your early life caregivers.

Oftentimes, when said child chooses to heal, grow, and move forward from their previous way of experiencing their relationships, the narcissistic parent will panic and begin to accuse the child of being "brainwashed" or lied to by the therapist/partner/friend/colleague who suggested they get help to heal their issues. For the parent, this means that they are no longer in control of their child and will have to suffer the consequences of that child's growth and preference to heal the wounds they incurred from the parent-child relationship.

A narcissistic parent might then distance themselves, choosing to reject and deny their child, hoping that their form of punishment will cause their offspring to "see the light" and return to their old dynamic. The parent is very telling in their behavior, as the child can now better see that all their parent wants is to serve their emotional needs and has no feeling for what their child has experienced.

Narcissistic parenting can cause a lot of issues in their child or children, and in adulthood, that child may learn the hard way what they were experiencing with their parent. To break it down further, here is a list of how a narcissistic parent can affect their children:

- The child will feel like they can't be heard or seen.

- They won't have their feelings acknowledged, or their reality validated.

- Rather than being seen as a person, they will be treated as the accessory to the parent.

- They won't be valued for who they are, only for what they can do, especially for the parent.

- The child will develop intense self-doubt, rather than learning to trust themselves and their identity.

- They will learn that how they feel it is less important and how they look is more important.

- They will learn that authenticity is not as good as an image and will then learn to be afraid of "being real" with others.

- The child will learn to behave and act secretively as a protection for the family or the parent.

- There will be no healthy encouragement to develop a sense of identity or self.

- They will not feel nurtured and can feel empty of emotions.

- They will learn that it is not good, or dangerous, to trust anyone.

- They will usually feel manipulated or used without understanding the feeling.

- The child will learn to "be there" for the parent, rather than how it should be when the parent is present and available for the child.

- Emotional development is stunted.

- They will feel judgment or criticism instead of unconditional love and acceptance.

- Feelings of not being good enough will develop.

- There will be no role model for creating healthy connections and relationship bonds.

- They will fail to learn healthy boundaries with others.

- They will learn to develop codependency and therefore, will not learn healthy self-care and self-love.

- They will be shown to seek validation from outside of the self instead of learning to validate the self from within.

- They will learn a mixed message of "make me proud" but also "don't do anything better than me."

- Will not learn to compliment the self or celebrate the self during important successes.

- May suffer from depression, addiction, anxiety, or other issues in adulthood to cope with the trauma of childhood.

- Will grow up assuming or believing that they are not lovable, or worthy of love because of the parent denying or rejecting them

- Will grow up with low self-esteem because of the shame in child-parent dynamics

- They will straddle a life of being someone who self-sabotages, overachieves, or fluctuating back and forth

- The child will have to learn the hard way how to reparent themselves once they break free from the parent-child dynamics in adulthood

The effects of being the child of a narcissist are intense, long-lasting, and deeply ingrained into the behaviors, emotions, and even physical qualities and attributes of a person. It can be psychologically and emotionally damaging and can lead to a lifetime of dealing with the programming instilled by the narcissistic parent during their child's formative years.

It can be difficult to tell that someone is a narcissist because of how charming they can be at the moment and how easy it is for them to get slippery as a fish when they are being questioned. They are very cunning, and even some psychologists can miss the red flags when they are being presented with a child's emotional or psychological pain.

Because a narcissist will never claim accountability or responsibility for their actions or behaviors, it then falls upon the child to take the brunt of the blame, guilt, shame, and remorse for anything that goes on. Every situation is different, as every family and every individual are different, but the red flags and hallmarks are the same. Review the above list to see if your child might have some of these symptoms, or if you can identify whether you may have been affected by a narcissistic parent when you were a child.

The opposite of narcissism is empathy. If you are in a situation with a child who is dealing with a narcissistic parent, then the best way to counter the damaging effects of the narcissist's abuse is to parent with empathy, offer compassion and support, and help to create a secure attachment so that the child in question can experience a healthy love bond that they can carry into their adult life.

It is important to remember that narcissism is a spectrum disorder and takes on varying degrees of severity. Whether you are the child of a narcissist, or you are in a relationship with one with whom you are trying to co-parent, it is important to understand this disorder so that you can help your whole family in healing, ending patterns and cycles, and breaking through to having healthier partnerships and bonds of love, for everyone involved.

Whether it is just for the sake of yourself, or perhaps your children as well, depending on the seriousness of the abuse and the effects on your happiness and well-being, letting go and moving on can feel scary, but this book is here to help offer you guidance as you explore and examine your options.

Chapter 9

_✦✦✦✦_

A Strict Set Of Rules

Rules are essential to the continuation of every narcissistic relationship. When leaving a narcissist, you'll likely receive a text or other form of communication along the lines of, "It's funny how you don't think you need to live by the rules. Just saying."

The 'rules' are their rules, and you don't need to live by them. No one has to live by a narcissist's warped set of rules. Narcissists and sociopaths, in general, have a certain set of rules their victims are expected to live by. These rules help to ensure control over their victims, that the dictatorship is kept alive and well.

Narcissistic rules can be enforced through covert or overt tactics, such as lies and manipulation as previously discussed, and through controlling behavior, and physical and mental abuse. The basic premise of all narcissist rules is that every action taken by the victim must appease the narcissist. The victim must think of the narcissist first. Spousal victims must give their narcissistic lover one-sided love, respect, and adoration at all times that will never be reciprocated. Don't expect it to be.

The effectiveness of the narcissist's rule-making and the enforceability of these rules rest in the victim's willingness to submit. All relationships have rules, per se. It's usually expected that a spouse remains faithful, that the couple has an open line of communication and lets each other know their whereabouts if they go somewhere unexpectedly. But, not only do narcissists refuse to abide by these basics, they take the setting of rules to the next level, and it's up to the victim to recognize the unhealthy ones inevitably established.

Controlling the way someone dresses, calling excessively and repeatedly, and putting alerts on cameras and devices informing the spouse of the whereabouts of their significant other at all times is not normal. Enforcing rules that have to do with obeying the narcissist is not normal. An example would be using a tool on their phone to be alerted every time a garage door is opened or setting up alerts on a joint bank account to be notified every time money is withdrawn even minuscule amounts. These things aren't accepted as normal by most individuals. They're non-physical, yet dangerous signs of narcissistic control.

Three additional and equally powerful rules the narcissist constructs early on, and need to be noted by a potential victim, are as follows:

- I can falsely accuse you of doing things you never did, and you are not allowed to make a liar out of me by defending yourself.

- You are not allowed to expose me and reveal the things I really did. You must cover up what I do and say and keep it a secret.

- You are never allowed to confront me. I'm the only one who is allowed to confront anybody.

Simply put, the narcissist expects their victim to suffer in silence. Any retaliation against their general, all-encompassing rule is a threat to the narcissist's false self and, therefore, simply unacceptable. The narcissist expects everything to roll off the back of their victim. Their behavior is 'no big deal' and not to be questioned. You're not allowed to hurt, to get angry, to be frustrated, or to feel pain. You must not only conceal any negative emotions you feel, you must shield your abuser from feeling discontented.

There are consequences for deviating from the rules. It's difficult to describe the wrath of a narcissist's rage if you've deviated from the rules to anyone who has not been through it first-hand, but victims know very well the dire effects.

Stealer of Ideas

One should never let a narcissist take over a project that is near and dear to their heart. The narcissist won't only take total control of the project, moving forward in whichever direction they choose, they'll dictate the entire process and upon completion, take full responsibility for its success, even claiming that it was all their idea. This is the same as asking a narcissist to go to couple's therapy. They'll likely refuse should their spouse make the suggestion until the stakes are high and they're about to lose everything, bring it up and blame the victim for not wanting to go—for giving up so easily.

It's unwise to do favors for narcissists, even if it's in one's nature to help others. The narcissist will take full advantage, asking more and more of that person until there is nothing left. When one finally says "no", they'll be called worthless or selfish.

If the narcissist asks someone to take on a project they will ultimately get credit for but is incapable of handling for one reason or another, this is absolutely a red flag. Ensuring its successful completion allows the narcissist to parade the rightful owner's accomplishment as their own as soon as the work is completed.

Lack of Empathy

Narcissists are incapable of possessing genuine empathy, even toward their own children. In fact, they don't feel commonplace emotions at all, especially those related to being at fault for causing hurt, such as guilt or remorse. But, as masters of manipulation, they take note of normal human emotions and are able to mirror them for their own benefit. For example, a narcissist witnesses a breakdown takes expert note of the accompanying behavior using their photographic memory, a common trait and files it away to mimic at a time that they deem beneficial. They're experts at analyzing human emotion, memorizing, and mimicking it, at will.

The narcissist mimics these behaviors while in the public eye to prove they're capable of caring for others. They may give generously to charitable organizations, advocate against world hunger or other societal issues and attend meetings, conferences, games, and other social events at their child's school. The one thing all of these efforts have in common is that they're done publicly for attention and for the benefit of the narcissist's reputation.

Narcissists are especially mindful of displaying empathy if they're attempting to attract a new mate. They prey on the vulnerable, often hand-picking unsuspecting abuse victims, promising to be their savior. Narcissists pretend to express empathy for their victims' trauma to solidify their position of power as the victim's 'knight in shining armor'. If they're still married or committed they'll disparage their current spouse or partner rather than attempting to hide it from their new target. They'll paint themselves as a victim and manipulate their new target to gain the empathy they crave.

A narcissist will go to great extremes to create an empathetic façade when attempting to attract a new partner. If the church serves as their hunting grounds of choice, which is common, they may hand-pick the most vulnerable member who is leaning on spirituality and the comfort of the church community to heal. The narcissist's presence in church creates a false persona of a good, moral person for their intended victim. They'll join the same groups as their target to get closer while studying and making note of what makes the victim tick. The narcissist may later use their position in the church to amplify the perception of perfection to others and increase their control the victim.

Narcissists are known to have 'picture' memories. They're highly skilled at taking mental images of their victims in the earliest stages, noting and committing to memory their appearance, clothing style, speech patterns, interests, and idiosyncrasies. This information gives the narcissist the knowledge and ability to make the victim believe they're everything they've ever wanted in a mate. Later the narcissist uses this knowledge to solidify the victim's sense of inadequacy. Once their initial study is complete, the narcissist makes their move.

Before inviting their victim over for the first time, the narcissist may replace their décor with religious art to aid in their deception. They may feign a keen interest in spirituality, publicly declaring their stance on social media. The more likes a narcissist gets the more their ego is fed and the more apt their victim is to accept the false persona. Once the victim is enthralled and the narcissist has complete control, the empathic behavior stops and their true personality is revealed.

If a victim is able to recognize the mirroring tactics and escapes the trap, going completely no contact, they'll start to identify the contortion they dealt with during the relationship. Over time, they'll recall each lie and each demonstration of false empathy, when something evokes a sudden memory of time with their abuser. This sudden recall of trauma at the hands of the narcissist is called Post-Traumatic Stress Disorder (PTSD), which is covered in more detail later in this work. PTSD generally requires professional treatment by a therapist for proper healing.

Mistreatment of Service Workers

Narcissists have a fervent need for attention and only enter into relationships when they know they'll benefit. Every relational arrangement is based on this premise. Even the briefest of encounters exist solely to serve their purpose. Superficial interactions, such as with a server at a restaurant, are not complicated by a deeper, more intimate connection. Therefore, the narcissism will surface much faster than it does when the narcissist wants to impress a potential mate. It's crucial to pay attention to their actions in these situations.

During the developmental stage of a relationship, it's helpful to note how your partner treats wait staff, flight attendants, grocery store cashiers, and other service employees. More than likely, if they're on the unhealthy narcissism scale, they'll treat these individuals with disrespect, just as they would anyone they deem inferior and decides their sole purpose is to wait on them hand and foot.

Chapter 10

How To Move On From The Narcissist

Ultimately, once you have escaped and begun to heal from the narcissist, you may be wondering how do you ever fully move on from the narcissist, particularly after he so thoroughly won your heart? It is definitely not an easy task, but if you have made it this far, you can do it. Moving on from the narcissist involves disengaging from the narcissist, practicing mindfulness, and bettering yourself. Through these skills, you will be able to distance yourself from the narcissist further, understand your feelings when you want to go back, and you can find a constructive way to use your feelings toward the narcissist.

With affirmations, you will have a tool in your back pocket to help you remember your value and what you want out of life.

Disengaging from the Narcissist

Disengaging from the narcissist will involve going through various stages, much like grieving. This is your process of letting go of the narcissist and recognizing that the relationship is ruined and needs to be ended permanently. Though easier said than done, disengaging and detaching from the narcissist is crucial to healing. Similar to the stages of grief, you will go through three distinct stages when you are attempting to disengage from the narcissist before finally reaching stage 4: freedom.

Stage 1: Refusing to take the blame

In stage 1, you refuse to allow yourself to be blamed for anything that happened. You tell yourself that you did not deserve what the narcissist did, and even though you may have ended the relationship, it was not you that degraded the relationship to the point that it had to be ended. This stage involves you recognizing that the narcissist will never give you what you deserved in the relationship. The narcissist will never be the partner you wanted him to be, and you recognize that. You acknowledge that the narcissist is flawed beyond your own ability to repair someone and that his destructive nature is not yours to manage, nor is it something that can be forced upon you. The narcissist becomes someone that you may love still, but you recognize the truth in the situation and that the relationship has to end for everyone's sake.

Stage 2: Anger and resentment

At stage 2, you realize that all of the hope you had for the relationship and the narcissist is being replaced. At this stage, you are angry. You see that the narcissist is not the person you wanted, and you begin to resent him. Even if you still have feelings at this stage, you are not likely to act upon them. Your eyes have been opened to the truth, and you refuse to allow the relationship to consume you any longer. At this stage, you no longer care about the manipulation the narcissist has likely been slinging at you to try to get you back. You really recognize that you deserve better than to be treated poorly or with disrespect. You feel the need to stand up for yourself and better yourself. You want to live a life of happiness, not one in which your sole duty is to provide someone else with the happiness you have been deprived of feeling for so long.

Stage 3: Detaching and setting yourself free

When you finally hit stage 3, you are finally detaching. The very sight of the narcissist or the mere mention of his name could be enough to make you feel sick to your stomach, and you realize that the love you had for him once upon a time has faded away. You have instead worked on bettering yourself. If you have been going to a therapist or been interacting with a support group, you are beginning to take their advice more frequently and realize that it works. You are far more concerned with getting what you want and need than worrying about the narcissist. You make your decisions based on what is best for you as opposed to anyone else, and for the first time in a long time, you can practically taste freedom.

Stage 4: Freedom

At this point, you are finally free. You no longer allow the narcissist to have any sway on you and you have likely cut all contact with him. You have completely and utterly separated yourself from the narcissist, and you could never feel better. Your freedom was earned through metaphorical, and quite possibly literal, blood, sweat, and tears, and you plan on enjoying it, no matter what the narcissist has to say about it.

Practicing Mindfulness

Mindfulness, at its simplest, is the idea that, when engulfed in chaos and strong emotions, you are able to take a moment to detach from the situation at hand and observe what is happening from a rational perspective. You sort of retreat within yourself to reflect on how you are feeling and why you are feeling the way you are in the hopes of finding answers that can help you better cope with what is bothering you.

This is a particularly useful way to identify any emotional triggers, those things in the outside world that automatically trigger you to feel everything the narcissist has programmed you to feel. There are undoubtedly some left in you after a relationship with a narcissist, but learning them all can take plenty of time and patience. When you want to practice mindfulness, you want to fully understand why you are responding the way you are.

This is a fantastic skill for anyone to have, as mindfulness can aid in controlling emotional outbursts, as well as help lessen stress. It is an incredibly healthy coping mechanism and is absolutely valuable to learn. Mindfulness involves five steps that will allow you to achieve the state of mindfulness. This state is a state of quiet, internal attentiveness. When you are first learning mindfulness, it is best to do so in periods of calmness to master the art before eventually beginning to use it when tensions run high.

Sit down

Step 1 in mindfulness is sitting down or identifying a quiet place in which you can quietly and safely focus on your breathing. Anywhere is acceptable, so long as you can focus and you are comfortable, so maybe try to find a quiet corner in your home, or underneath a tree in your yard. The important part here is that you need to be calm and relaxed wherever you choose.

Choose a time

With the goal in mind, choose how long you are willing to dedicate to your first few attempts at mindfulness. Typically, you are better off starting with a shorter period at first and slowly working your way up to longer ones. Perhaps, for your first time, set a goal of 5 minutes of mindfulness.

Pay attention to your body

Choose a comfortable position and really focus on your body. You want to choose a position in which you feel stable and relaxed, and that will be comfortable for the duration of your mindfulness. Once you have settled in, really start to focus on your body. Attempt to feel every part of yourself, starting at the tips of your toes and slowly working your way up to the top of your head. You should do this slowly as if you were mentally scanning yourself. Pay attention to any areas that are particularly tense and try to relax them.

Breathe

Focus on your breathing. Take one breath in and try to follow the feeling of it all the way into your lungs, holding it there before exhaling, and repeating. Make sure your breaths are deep, cleansing breaths, and really focus on each one.

Keep your mind on track

Any time you feel your mind wandering, quietly put it back on your breathing without judging yourself. Remember how you are supposed to feel compassionate about yourself? This is a good place to start! Particularly, in the beginning, it is easy to get distracted, and that is nothing to be ashamed of. Just regroup and continue.

After completing all the steps, you should feel far more relaxed than when you started. This can be a fantastic tool to use to unwind after a busy or stressful day, or when you feel your temper rising. As you master being able to call yourself to mindfulness when calm, you can begin using it as a coping mechanism when you feel frustrated or stressed out, or any time you start to debate whether returning to the narcissist would really be too bad. Oftentimes, those insecurities are tied to some sort of physical distress, and you should try to let them go as best as you can.

Another trick for mindfulness that some people find works well, particularly when emotions are running high is the 5-4-3-2-1 rule. In this technique, you seek to identify things around you with your various senses, engaging them instead of allowing your negative emotion to consume you, and when you focus on yourself again, you are better able to manage your own reactions in the future.

Sight

First, start by identifying five things around you that you can see. Be as descriptive as possible with yourself if you can be. Perhaps you see a blue ball with a woven texture on the ground, smooth, clear glass on the table next to you, and a sky the color of a clear blue ocean that you dream about vacationing to see. When you have identified five things to yourself, you are ready to move on to your next sense

Touch

Next, focus on your sense of touch. Notice four different things around you that you can feel. Perhaps you feel sand giving way beneath your feet, or a cool breeze caressing your hair. Whatever you feel, try to identify four as specifically as possible. Really feel each one the best you can, and focus on every single detail. Notice how your hair tickles your face when the wind blows it, or how your entire body shifts as the sand does beneath you, compensating for the moving surface.

Hear

You should then focus on your hearing. Listen for three things around you and really take a few moments to hear them. You should pay attention to how they sound, following their melodies and rhythms the best you can. If you hear a bird trilling, focus on how its song rises and falls and how quickly it does.

Smell

Fourth, you will identify two different things around you that you can smell. Do you smell your perfume? What is the scent you have this time? Is it sweet? Musky, do you smell the scents of flowers warming in the sun? Try to identify as many elements of the scent as you can.

Feeling

Lastly, identify one thing within you that you are feeling at that moment. Are you angry? What is that anger doing to your body? Is it speeding your pulse up? Is it making you tense up? If you are sad, do you feel that hollow feeling spreading in your chest? Are your shoulders hunched? Figure out how you are feeling and how it affects your body.

With your mindfulness achieved, you will better be able to deal with whatever emotions your body was reacting to, choosing healthy, rational reactions as opposed to exploding or acting with emotional impulses.

Bettering Yourself

As you continue on your journey toward getting over the narcissist, you should put work into yourself. Attempting to better yourself gives you something else entirely to focus on, aside from the narcissist and will keep you busy. You will not have time to worry about the narcissist as much if you pick up a new hobby, such as learning to play the piano. You can even use this hobby to insert into time that you usually spent with the narcissist. For example, if you always spent Friday nights together eating takeout and watching your narcissist's favorite television program that you always secretly hated, you could instead use that weekly allotment of time to work on your new skill. Perhaps you choose this evening time to work on scales or try to learn the new songs your piano teacher has assigned for the week. Maybe instead, you look up video tutorials on how to play all sorts of songs that you listen to that remind you to stay strong.

Ultimately, learning a new skill and bettering yourself can only help you. You will never be worse off if you focus your energy and attention on learning a new skill, but if you use that time to focus on the past, dwell, and mope, you are likely to feel guilty about it later. Overall, it just makes more sense for you to spend that time focusing on things that will better you or can give you some new sense of self-worth to replace the damage the narcissist has done.

Affirmations

One last useful skill to learn when trying to get over the narcissist is learning how to form proper affirmations. An affirmation is a small sentence you use to remind yourself of an objective or goal or to reaffirm your own boundaries. They are usually quite short and are a common part of many different therapies, including cognitive-behavioral therapy, which teaches those who are using it to restructure their thinking. The idea here is to reverse the damage that the narcissist has done to you through all of his cruel words and demeaning comments. You listened to his cruelties for so long that you internalized them, and affirmations seek to do the exact opposite using the same concept. You will repeat your affirmations to yourself so often that you will convince yourself that they are true. Over time, you will begin to believe them, just like you believed the narcissist's disparaging comments. Affirmations have three key parts to them: They must be positive, self-directed, and present tense.

Positive

The reason you want to focus your affirmation on the positive is that it will shift your entire way of thinking. You will feel more positively if you think more positively. This uses the idea that you attract what you think. Think of it this way—in cognitive behavioral therapy; it is recognized that thoughts influence behaviors, which influence feelings, which influence thoughts, and the cycle continues. If you have a positive thought, it will lead to positive behavior, which will create a positive feeling, which will then create more positive thoughts. Positivity breed positivity, and ultimately, that can present itself all over your life. Your positivity will spread throughout your life, starting with that one simple positive affirmation, just as the narcissist's negativity spread through you.

Self-directed

Your affirmation must focus on yourself because ultimately, the only thing in this world you really have complete control over is yourself. When you are talking about yourself, you cannot come up with a way to deny its truth if you are thinking it. By focusing on yourself, you can make it come true. If you say that you will breathe before reacting to tense situations, you have the influence to make that happen. That is the important part here—you make it happen. If your affirmation focused on anyone else, you could not guarantee its validity, nor do you have any control over whether it happens. This makes it difficult to really trust or rely on.

Present tense

The reason for a present tense affirmation is that saying it at the moment prompts it to be true at that moment. If you say that you will do something, it is ambiguous whether that means immediately or sometime in the future. It is easier to sidestep that problem altogether and keep the affirmation present tense.

With these three rules in mind, you are ready to create your affirmations. You take all three aspects and stick them together to create a sentence like:

- I deserve to be treated with respect, dignity, and kindness.

- I am enough the way that I am right now.

- The way I see the world is trustworthy, and I always trust my perceptions of what is happening around me.

Each of these affirmations provides some sort of guidance and prompts you to believe in yourself more. You can create affirmations for virtually any situation that you think would benefit from them, and you should use them whenever you feel they would help. At the very least, make it a point to recite each affirmation to yourself at least ten times a day at the same time every day to make it a habit. For example, you could tell yourself, "I am enough the way that I am right now," every time you sit down in the car to drive to work. Every day, you repeat it several times to yourself, and eventually, that thought becomes just as reflexive and habitual as putting your seatbelt on when you get into your car. This is how you slowly shift your mind from the one poisoned by the narcissist into the healthier one you deserve.

Chapter 11

─────── ❧❦❧❦❧ ───────

Living With One, Dealing With One

Although it is said that only one percent of the population is considered to have Narcissism, you can encounter Narcissists in many different situations. They are hard to deal with, especially if you are in a personal relationship with them. If the Narcissist is a member of your family or your partner, it is considered one of the toughest situations to deal with. Narcissists often have ulterior motives when talking to someone and sometimes they can even be cruel because they don't really care about the other person's feelings. Let's see what ways a Narcissist can influence your life and tips that you can use.

Dealing With Narcissists You Live And Work With (Tips Included)

If you are living with Narcissistic parents, there is a fair chance that you will end up as a Narcissist too. Some scientists believe that Narcissism can be passed down through genetics too. Genetic link could be a cause, but more often the reason is the way the child is raised. We already mentioned that Narcissistic parents are not the best at raising children. They usually focus on their own needs and have really high expectations of how the child should perform. The child becomes a reflection of the parent and gives the parent the sought after attention. When we were talking about the consequences of being raised in Narcissistic families, we saw that some of those parents ignore their children, only talking to them when it benefits them in some way. Children live a life full of drama and they learn how to suppress and cut off their emotions. The Narcissistic parent doesn't really understand the feelings that their child is going through, so they just don't pay attention to it, they ignore it, which is why many of these children are ignored and abused. If the child; however, tries to do something that the parent doesn't like, it can end up being a big problem. The parent can belittle and humiliate the child until they agree with the parent. Children raised by Narcissistic parents usually have trouble forming a connection with others because they never formed a proper attitude towards feelings. On the contrary, they shut them down because it wasn't desirable to have emotions that don't meet their parents' needs. They are mimicking the behavior that they saw in their parents because those were their role models. As they were growing up, thinking about others wasn't something that they would even consider. If you think that you were raised by Narcissistic parents, maybe you could talk to a trained professional to help you out. Even if you don't have Narcissistic Personality Disorder yourself, it is good to have somebody to share your worries with.

If you are living with a Narcissistic spouse it can be really hard. First of all, you've spent some time building up a relationship with this person. Then, if the kids came and you even purchased a home, you have basically built up your whole life around them. Many people are charmed by Narcissists without even realizing it because the Narcissist can certainly be persuasive and know how to manipulate the situation to get what they want. Since they are addicted to attention, as long as you give the Narcissist the attention that he wants and he wants to get something from you, the Narcissist is going to be your best friend. The problem starts when he's done needing you or if you start disagreeing with him. If you ever got into a fight with the Narcissist, you probably felt used and demeaned. You later realized that no good agreement came from it and it's because a Narcissist has a way of putting things to his own accordance. You may end up dealing with the Narcissist for a long time, for many years even. They can keep up their charming behavior for a long time and, especially if you are living together, it becomes easy to excuse the Narcissist's occasional destructive behavior as having a bad day at work or believing that you were the one who caused the issue. By the time you realize that you are dealing with a Narcissist, you are already having a long life built around him and it is hard to get away.

If you are living with a Narcissistic friend, it can be especially hard to deal with it. It can be that you've known this person for your whole life and maybe there were some situations that you felt like you should cut that person off because they don't treat you well. And even if you tried to do so, your Narcissistic friend came back, repented, and was even more charming than before. This is a standard Narcissistic technique because that person wants you to give him attention or is terrified by the thought of being alone. That kind of friend will always come back telling you that he's sorry for the way he has acted and, basically, beg you to come back to. If you thought about breaking off a friendship because that person doesn't seem to care about your feelings and you feel like they're using you, you are most likely dealing with a Narcissist. Like any Narcissist, this person is also really good at keeping someone around if they want them. This kind of friend will do and say anything to keep you around to make them feel good, so if you try to break it off with them, they will start behaving awful. While these people can be charming and amazing when you first meet them, they can also be your worst nightmare when they want something. If you feel like you are always being used or you get in big fights whenever you offend your friend, that means that he is a Narcissist and the thing is that during those fights, they can never even take the blame. As long as everything is going according to their plan and wishes, things will go well. But if things start to change and to stray from the Narcissist's plans, that means trouble. If you have this kind of friend, you should consider a way to break off from them. Try limiting the contact. Maybe slowly at first, that can be a small but a good step. You should also consider finding people who will look after you and be there to support you.

If you have a Narcissistic boss or coworker it is can be tricky and it can influence you on multiple levels. If you enjoy the job you do and it happens that you have a Narcissistic boss or coworker, it can be particularly hard to deal with them and you will have to work hard. There are; however, some things that you can do that can make your life easier.

You should try not to take their promises seriously. If your Narcissist boss or coworker wants you to do something for him or her, they are going to sweet-talk you. If you take their talk seriously, you can get disappointed. If you learn how to recognize Narcissists and you realize what they are trying to do, you will understand that as soon as the promise is inconvenient for the Narcissist, they will act like the promise they made never existed You also should never try, and waste your oxygen, telling the Narcissist that he is wrong. From their point of view, they can't be wrong. Never. They believe that they are more superior to others and if you confront them, they will act as an enemy. The best way to deal with them is to just ignore them. Try and ignore their charm too. Like we mentioned several times, Narcissists can be very charming people when they want something. If they can gain something from you, they are going to be your best friend and they will try to use their charm on you. Once the Narcissist gets what he wants, he stops being so friendly and excludes you quickly when he loses interest.

You need to establish who the enablers are. A Narcissist, especially if they are a boss and have gained some power, will surround himself with people who will do anything for him. His endless need for supremacy and desire to manipulate will make him treat other people like puppets for his needs. If you don't want to become one of these people, you will need to establish who the enablers are and to start working with them. This way you will get what you want. For example, if you have a Narcissistic boss and you want a raise, you will ask someone who is close to the Narcissist to help you out with this. This enabler will be even more useful if the Narcissist needs a favor from them.

They say that there aren't many Narcissists in the world; however, as soon as one gets into your life, it can be difficult for you to get rid of them. The Narcissist regularly wants to keep you around so that they can get all the attention they want or they just need you to fulfill another need for them. They will in no way do something for you unless it is going to benefit them in some way. There is never a time when they will do something that will concern you or your well being and they'll never do something for you just because of the fact they are your friend. The truth is that you can use some techniques and strategies to deal with a Narcissist. If nothing else, they will help you deal with them and will make you extra prepared when they come around.

Techniques And Strategies

- You need to determine the type of Narcissist you are dealing with. How you deal with each type is different also. A vulnerable Narcissist, for example, doesn't have the highest self-esteem, but the grandiose Narcissist will push everyone and everything over to get what they want. If you need to make an ally of the Narcissist, the grandiose Narcissist is the best choice, you just need to convince him that the goal benefits him as well.

- You should acknowledge that you are annoyed. It is common that a Narcissist will get under your skin. If you feel frustrated because whenever you start doing something, the Narcissist goes around interrupting you and wanting all the attention, you should admit and acknowledge that frustration. It will help you deal with the Narcissist later.

- You need to appreciate where the behavior comes from. When you understand how Narcissists feel and why they act as they do, it might not help you accept it but it can help you deal with it. If you establish and understand that the Narcissist isn't considering other people's emotions because he is incapable of feeling empathy, it will be easier for you to avoid being caught up with them or influenced by them.

- You should keep your expectations realistic. Narcissists will always have limitations on their emotions. It is important to remember that even if it is fine to enjoy some good qualities that come with a Narcissist. If you learn to accept that their emotions are limited, it will help you to stop asking and expecting something that they can't provide.

- It is especially important that you don't make your self-worth dependent on them! If you do that, it is just going to make you feel bad in the end. People often fall into a trap of trying to make the Narcissist happy. But the Narcissist won't be happy no matter how hard you try. Don't try to confide your deepest secrets and desires to the Narcissist because they won't take it seriously or cherish them and will probably use them against you at some point if they feel like they need to.

- You should try to turn something to their benefit. If you want to learn how to successfully communicate with a Narcissist, you need to understand that you always have to show him how it will benefit him. Talking about your own needs is not going to work with the Narcissist and being demanding or acting angry won't work either. Instead, you should show the Narcissist how you can be helpful to the Narcissist so that they will consider helping you.

To be able to deal with Narcissists requires a lot of patience, learning, and self-management. Since they don't react to situations as most people do, you can't go and use conventional methods to deal with them. While others may be around you or work with you because they feel something about you or because they want to help, the Narcissist is not going to understand how that works. He is going to do things according to his own beliefs which are not based on common behavior.

Dealing With A Narcissist You Love

When you are in love with a Narcissist, or in a relationship with one, it can be very hard to see what your next steps are going to be. When you deal with the Narcissist at work or if it is your neighbor, you can consider leaving your job, finding a new one, and just stop communication. If you have a friend who has Narcissistic traits, you can just try and find another group of friends. But what to do when the Narcissistic person is someone you've been with for years? Someone who you have kids with and who you love? There are many challenges that people need to go through when they have a relationship with a Narcissist and there are a lot of reasons that they consider too important to break off that relationship.

The hard part is realizing that you are living with a Narcissistic spouse. First of all, you love this person. And what if you have a family and kids with this person? What if you have built a life with them? When you think about it, changing jobs sounds easy. Finding a new group of friends sounds easier too. Still, there are a few techniques and strategies that can help with Narcissistic spouse or partner.

Techniques And Strategies

- You need to be safe, as some Narcissists tend to turn to abuse when they are not able to get what they want, but this is not the case with all Narcissists. However, if you are dealing with abuse that is a product of Narcissistic behavior, it is time that you finish that relationship.

- You need to give yourself permission to think about yourself and not always be thinking about your partner and putting him first. Narcissists are very good at convincing you to think about them all the time but you need to reconnect with yourself and try to meet your own needs.

- Never forget to remind yourself of your own self-worth! Narcissists always try to belittle you so they can feel superior and have the admiration that they want. You need to find a way to always remind yourself that you are smart, lovable, and deserving; even if your partner might tell you otherwise.

- Learn how to deal with your insecurities. Use all the resources that you can get to help deal with any insecurities that you might have. It doesn't matter if those insecurities were provoked by your Narcissistic partner or if they are something that you are dealing with from before. Your insecurities make you more vulnerable and you need to learn how to overcome them.

- You need to accept that you are not able to change your partner. The main reason for this is that usually, the Narcissist doesn't see a reason to change. He doesn't see a problem because from the way that he sees it - everything is normal. Don't forget that people with Narcissistic Personality Disorder have a twisted image of being normal.

- You also need to accept that that kind of behavior is about the other person. You are not the one to blame and you don't need to feel guilty or try to justify the other person. If you feel like your partner or spouse has Narcissistic traits, you should consider sharing what's going on to a friend or some other person of confidence. You should consider what you see as unacceptable behavior and if your attitude about it has changed since you started to be with your

Narcissistic partner. You should also determine if you've been making up excuses for your partner.

- Once you decide what the right boundaries are, tell your partner about it. You shouldn't expect that this kind of initiative will go without consequences. The Narcissistic partner will probably just ignore all your requests and will refuse to follow any boundaries. If you decide to do this, you need to prepare yourself to leave if there isn't anything else that you can do.

If you realize that you are in a relationship with a Narcissist, you need to learn how to accept that you need to end that relationship.

Can A Narcissist Change?

At this point, the cure for Narcissistic personality disorder doesn't exist. The only way that people with this disorder can get help is through individual, family, or group therapy. However, the most efficient form of therapy for this disorder is Cognitive-Behavioral Psychotherapy (CBT). The reason why CBT is the most successful treatment, is that it helps the Narcissist to understand their negative behaviors and replace their negative beliefs with positive ones.

The Narcissist won't change completely, but he can build more constructive behavior and they can get to the point where they understand the negative effects they cause. Keep in mind that not every Narcissist can change. That is why is important to determine which type of Narcissist are you dealing with, or what type of Narcissist you are. A Narcissist maybe can't change, in terms of science, but he can learn to build more realistic expectations toward others and himself. He can also learn how to relate more positively to other people.

Tips That Can Help You With The Change

- As we already mentioned, keep in mind that different types of Narcissists have a different motivation, thus different ability to change their behavior. Try to determine the type and see who you are really dealing with

- Narcissists don't have an insight into their negative traits; therefore they see themselves as superior that is why it is even harder to make them realize negative aspects of their personality. This is where therapists can help the most. They will make the Narcissist realize the point of view of others.

- This is also associated with the fact that Narcissistic positive self-perception is stronger than others' perceptions and reputation.

- You need to make Narcissists realize that they are Narcissistic since they usually aren't aware of that. In most of the cases, they don't even realize that others don't see them as glorious as they see themselves

- If normal methods don't work, you need to keep in mind that some Narcissists search for help if they feel desperate or anxious. If they face constant failures in their workplace or with their partners, it is likely that they will be willing to go to therapy.

- If a Narcissist is able to acknowledge a weakness, that is also a good sign and he is on the path of recovery, and he will tend to invest more in his personal growth.

- Last but not least, be mindful of the reasons for a Narcissist to change. It is easier to help them if they do it for their own benefit. As you know, Narcissist won't do anything for anyone else, so instead of asking "do it for my sake", consider convincing them that a change of their behavior will benefit them very much.

Conclusion

Thank you for making it through to the end. The next step is to focus on healing and rebuilding your sense of self. Narcissistic abuse can teach victims unhealthy coping mechanisms, such as unwarranted defensiveness, numbing the self to emotional experiences, or self-medicating to dull emotional pain. These legacies of the abuse will need to be confronted, examined, and dismantled in order to free yourself entirely.

If private therapy isn't readily available to you, remember that there are lots of other resources out there designed specifically for abuse victims, adult children of narcissists, and people who have escaped cult-like groups or institutions. Support groups can be immensely healing, whether they are found in physical or virtual spaces. If you're unable to find one in your area, it might make sense to look into starting one up. Narcissistic abuse can lead victims to feel lonely and isolated, even when they are surrounded by love; but internet search data tells us that the problem of narcissistic abuse is indeed widespread. You will never know how many other people understand your experience, and have survived similar forms of abuse, until you reach out to share your story.

No matter who you may turn to in search of validation, never forget to honor yourself in your healing practice. You deserve recognition; you deserve respect; you deserve love. And if others do not offer you these things, you are fully entitled to bestow them upon yourself.

www.ingramcontent.com/pod-product-compliance
Lightning Source LLC
Chambersburg PA
CBHW071233020426
42333CB00015B/1455